Traces of War

Survivors of the Burma and Sumatra Railways

Traces of War

Survivors of the Burma and Sumatra Railways

Jan Banning

* * TROLLEY * *

Contents

Looking For a Hidden Past

An Introduction
Jan Banning

In the rear mirror, Vukovar's last ruins soon disappear. A single
Serb or Croat is still seen sauntering along the pockmarked road.
I've just finished my assignment photographing and interviewing
people belonging to either segment of the population in the
ruined Croatian city. Now, on the way back, I'm wondering how
this fits in with my work thus far. Recalling several previous
projects, it suddenly becomes obvious what they have in common:
I've covered veterans of the Spanish Civil War; the consequences
of Agent Orange in Vietnam; war veterans in psychiatric institutions in that same country; victims of land mines in Cambodia;
and similar subjects, all of them having to do with the long-term
consequences of war.

    Why do people do the things they do? Why this subject
while I myself was raised in times of peace? Looking for an answer,
I quickly arrived at the vicissitudes of my parents: Both had been
born in the Dutch East Indies, where war had abruptly shattered
their happy and prosperous youth. In various ways, that war signified the collapse of their secure existence. It had left an indelible
impression on them. Freedom and security had been replaced by the
grim bondage of, in my mother's case, life in an internment camp,
and, in my father's case, forced labor. Prosperity and privacy quickly became a thing of the past. Families were broken up and scat-
tered to camps for men, camps for women and children and camps
for boys, often without any knowledge of each other's fate. The end
of the war didn't bring peace but a new threat: No joyous liberation
but banishment to an alien and chilly country, the Netherlands.

    I can't quite recall when I was confronted first with my par-
ents' Indies past. I do remember that it was for my mother always
a common topic in conversation. For as long as I can remember,
I was at least vaguely aware that my parents were "from somewhere
else." In the company of old friends, they would suddenly begin
to utter exotic sounds, drop mysterious names, and start rolling
their Rs. Conversations not meant for small ears were conducted
in Malay. We children learned a smattering of words that lost their
meaning the moment we stepped outside the house. Without any

roots anywhere in the Netherlands, our family moved all over the place. Whenever I looked at the other children with their colorful collection of nicknames, all snugly at home in the towns and villages we only passed through, I knew one thing for sure: We were different.

At some stage, although I am not sure when, the subject of internment camps reared its head. If the subject ever was surrounded by the silence of taboo, that silence was lifted as years passed. We were often told that my mother had once again been dreaming about that period. Often these were funny stories, which she dished up during meal times, and the subject mostly involved "outsmarting the Japs." But reading between the lines, it became obvious to me that not everything had been fun and games.

Gradually, my mother became more explicit on the subject, especially when we asked. And slowly, around his retirement, my father also began to open up. For the first time we heard something about his having been a prisoner of war, and about the Sumatra Railway, where he'd been a forced laborer. We also heard vague references to grandfather, who had been put to work on the railway in Burma. Once, while spending a few days at home, I noticed the steadily growing collection of books about the Indies, including Henk Hovinga's *Dodenspoorweg door het oerwoud* ("Railway of Death through the Jungle"),[1] dealing with my father's railroad. Reading the book gave me an "in," so to speak, to ask questions. I began to see some things in a different light, such as my parents' frugality and their obsessive saving of even unappetizing leftovers.

In the years following, my mother wrote down details about her Indies youth, including her time spent in the internment camp. I also had many talks, long ones, with my father that included his war experiences and in which he discussed things openly.

As such, as years went by, their war was securely embedded in my consciousness, not as a burden but simply as a given, and quite possibly as an addition to my overall wisdom. And apparently this also manifested itself in the choice of subjects in my work. When I finally realized this influence, dealing with it in a deliberate fashion seemed the logical thing to do.

1   The book's fourth edition is now entitled Eindstation Pakan Baroe 1943-1945 ("Pekanbaru Terminal 1943-1945").

Both my parents seemed to have come out of that period relatively unscathed, perhaps in part because neither of them lost any family. Homesickness seemed to be their biggest heartache. But I had become aware meanwhile of the painful silence that many of their peers maintained and wondered what was going through those people's minds. What possibly had been on my taciturn grandfather's mind – his silence in such sharp contrast to my now talkative father? How much of a burden was the legacy of the war to others? Were they still haunted by visions of the past? And to what extent did they think the war had determined who they were and what they thought and felt today?

Meanwhile, my mother had passed away. But my father was still alive, so him I could still observe and ask questions. He and his fellow war veterans roughly shared the same experiences. But was their legacy of the war comparable?

It took me a long time before I found a format that made sense. The questions I asked couldn't be answered with photographic means only, but I consider myself a photographer first and foremost and looked, therefore, for a visual way to express myself – something beyond simply photo-journalistic registration. That only emerged after allowing ample time for listening, reading and thinking. I had to take these men back visually to the time of forced labor, a time when they worked dressed in nothing but a *tjawat*, a small loincloth, with their chests bare. After extensive deliberations among our Indies acquaintances about its propriety, I decided that this would be my photographic point of departure. After all, both the photographs and the interviews had to connect and relate the past – the experiences from that era – to the present time: What are the traces of that war?

The first candidate I asked was my father, a willing subject. The others I traced through him, through the ever-helpful Henk Hovinga, through the journal *Pelita Nieuws*,[2] and by word of mouth. A few men withdrew after initially consenting because the prospect of a photograph and interview session was enough to bring on night-mares and other distress. Two men were prompted by their wives and children to withdraw for fear of how it would affect the men. But the others understood the reason behind the photographic approach and agreed to cooperate.

During his accounts of the Sumatra period, my father would time and again mention the fate of the *romushas*. These were forced civilian laborers of Asian extraction, many Indonesians among them,

whose fate had been much harsher still than my father's and his
fellow POWs. Hundreds of thousands of romushas also had worked
on those railroads, far more, therefore, than the estimated 66,000
white and Indo-European soldiers. A great many of these Asians
had succumbed and had been buried in unmarked graves or thrown
out like trash. When my parents, during a sentimental journey to
Sumatra, came upon a story on that subject in a local Padang news-
paper, my father right away sought contact with its author. He got
to meet this Makmur Hendrik, who, it turned out, had written a
whole series of stories about these men.

Eighteen years later, out of a sense of justice, I definitely
wanted to include romushas in my project. Insofar as the forced
labor on the railroads gets any attention at all in the West – like,
for example, in the movie *The Bridge on the River Kwai* – it's virtually always about the white prisoners of war only. People of
Dutch-Indonesian extraction rarely are noticed, and the romushas never seem to enter the picture at all. This is, incidentally,
true in Indonesia as well, probably because the involvement
of Sukarno, the hero of Indonesian independence, in the shady
recruitment of romushas. All this makes it one hell of a challenge
to trace these men.

My hopes rested with Makmur Hendrik. He proved traceable;
he had by then moved to Pekanbaru, where the Sumatra Railway
once began, and seemed pleasantly surprised by my interest. He
twice printed an invitation in his publication urging former romushas to come forward, to which four men had responded shortly
before my arrival. Two of them had indeed worked as a romusha
on the Sumatra Railway. One of them, *pak* Nur,[3] lived no less than
12 hours travel away, someplace toward Singapore. Apparently,
he didn't want to run the risk that I might decide against a trip to
the boondocks. The day after I arrived in Pekanbaru with my friend
and translator Monique Soesman, Makmur told us that pak Nur was
on his way. He was willing to talk, that much was clear.

Subsequently we traveled to the second volunteer, pak
Samlawi. On the way to Telukkuantan, where he lived, we followed
the route of the long-since vanished railway. We regularly stopped

2   A publication for victims of the war in the Dutch Indies.

3   Pak means mister or father, the customary way to address an elderly gentleman.

    Many Indonesians bear one name only.

in villages along the way to inquire after other surviving forced laborers. And lo and behold, after having been told several times *semua sudah mati*, "all dead already," a cheerful boy on a scooter approached us in Logas, which used to be a maintenance center for the railroad. "Hello, my name is Ronny. How can I help you?" "We're looking for romushas," we replied in a somewhat petulant tone. "My neighbor," Ronny said. And sure enough "Grandpa Sweet Potato" Damin turned out to be a former romusha. And he wasn't the only one in Logas, either. There were two more living romushas, pak Sardi and pak Sineng. They, too, didn't hesitate much to tell their story, and they were willing to pose as well, even if that meant clearing out the living room.

On Java, I had been promised help by the *LBH*, the office of legal aid in Yogya. Two of the men working there, pak Suratno and pak Sudibyo, had promised to do some scouting for me in the nearby but inaccessible area called Gunung Kidul. Traveling in an old car, then by scooter, and finally on foot, they managed to track down three romushas willing to accompany them back to Yogya. In a hot and cramped hotel room we conduced interview sessions for hours on end. Of the three, only pak Sidul spoke Indonesian fluently, while pak Ngadiyo and pak Ngadari required translation from Javanese to Bahasa Indonesia first. Finally, after returning to Jakarta, someone got me in touch with George Voorneman, an Indonesian former POW who spoke Dutch.

By now, a large part of the Burma Railroad has fallen into disrepair or has been dismantled. As for the Sumatra Railroad, the rusty remains of a few locomotives can still be seen in some forgotten corners of central Sumatra, such as a shabby suburb of Pekanbaru and in the jungle somewhere near Lipatkain. Otherwise, there are hardly any traces left of these men-devouring enterprises. But the memories of them, which at first seemed locked away so well in the deepest dungeons of the human mind, almost 60 years later still appear to be rattling their chains regularly.

To many people in the Netherlands, this period has always been a bit murky. Now, after so many years, it seems all the more necessary to provide a context that allows for the proper understanding of the individual accounts. Hence the introductory article by Esther Captain and Henk Hovinga, two authors who are very familiar with the era of Japanese occupation in Indies history. At the end of this book, Wim Willems, another expert on Indies history and a photography buff, provides context and interprets this project in a personal essay.

The stories make up the mid section of the book. They were actually told before the photographs were taken. The interviews generally lasted between two and six hours. Recorded in their entirety, they were subsequently transcribed and, of course, condensed for this book. Each interview has a reference to the accompanying portrait.

The first 15 stories are by Dutchmen, all of them former POWs. Next is George Voorneman, also a former POW but an Indonesian national. The eight stories of the Indonesian romushas complete the series. Of the 24 men, 10 worked on the Burma Railway, two of them as romushas. The remaining 14, six romushas among them, were at the Sumatra Railway. Their portraits are separated from the stories to provide space for both and to make sure the photographs aren't reduced to mere illustrations trudging behind the stories.

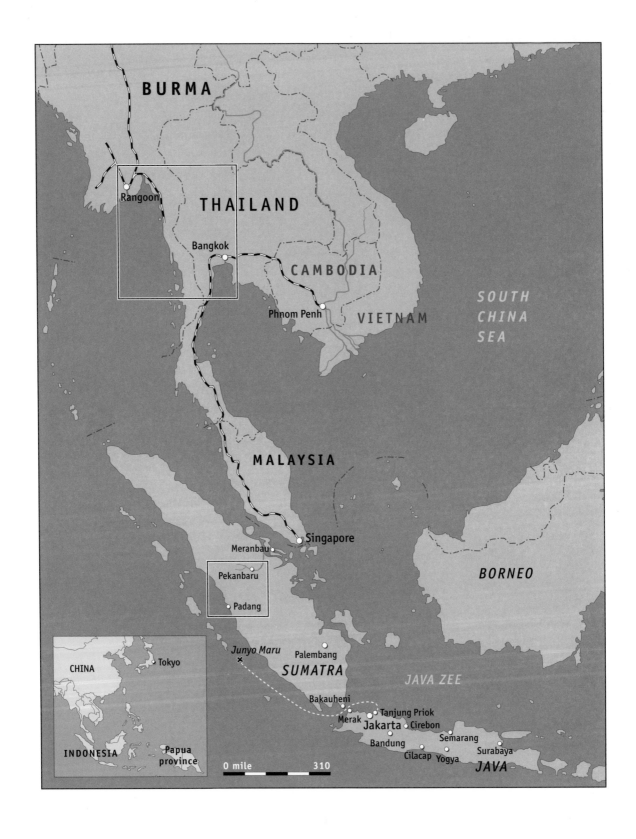

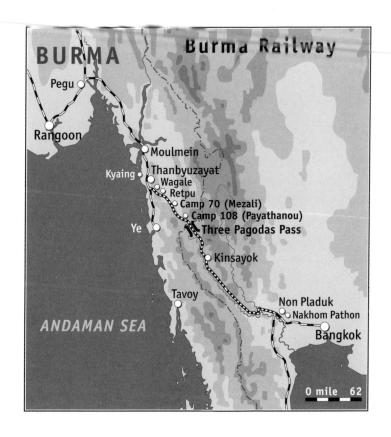

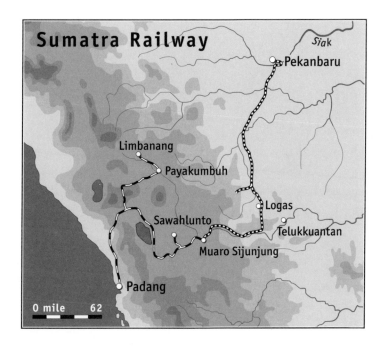

Retracing the War

An Historical Introduction
Esther Captain and Henk Hovinga

The 24 men in this book all have very different memories of the time when they were put to work on either the Burma or the Sumatra Railway as a prisoner of war or as a *romusha*, a civilian forced laborer of Asian extraction. Some have little difficulty with the past and deny the notion of victimization or of hatred against the Japanese, even though they acknowledge the miserable circumstances at the time, and even though the many who died are forever etched in their memory. Others are haunted often by what happened in the camps. As in a ritual, tormenting thoughts and spirits visit one of them at set times early in the morning. To protect themselves, some men have a "Rambo dagger" on their bedside table or a *klewang*, a machete, under their bed. Their family members have been warned never to enter their bedroom unannounced, "for then there's a chance that something might happen." The still-present reflex is: "They won't get me!" What kind of world did these men live in? How did the Asian civilian forced laborers and the allied POWs end up working on these infamous railways?

The Burma Railway was built between July 1942 and October 1943 and subsequently maintained until August 1945. The Sumatra or Pekanbaru Railway was built between April 1943 and August 1945. The construction of the Burma and Sumatra Railways were part of the Japanese war effort. The official aim of the Japanese occupation of other Asian countries was to create a so-called "Greater Asian Co-Prosperity Sphere," administered,

to be sure, by the land of the Rising Sun. The Japanese invasion of Manchuria in 1931 may be regarded as the historical start of their imperial, military expansionism.

The Japanese ambition to become the leading nation in all of Southeast Asia was based on that country's belief in its superiority over the traditional, western colonial powers. Even so, the Japanese war cabinet realized very well that lasting military domination could only be guaranteed if their country, lacking important resources, could have access to substantial militarily strategic goods and supplies. Particularly oil was of strategic importance. Well before the war finally broke out, Japan, in endless negotiations with the United States and the Dutch East Indies, tried to secure uninterrupted delivery of strategically important goods and minerals. Those negotiations came to a definitive halt on June 17, 1941, in Batavia, present-day Jakarta. The government of the Dutch East Indies refused to give in to the Japanese demands for particularly the supply of oil. The same happened shortly thereafter in the United States, which even declared a total oil embargo starting July 25. On December 1 of that year, the American oil embargo was followed by a general trade embargo. The Dutch government, then in exile in London, followed suit, military threats notwithstanding. Japan had, after all, in addition to large parts of China, already occupied all of Indochina.

The allied embargoes as well as the freezing of Japanese assets abroad proved to be an enormous setback for Tokyo. The Japanese war cabinet had more or less counted on particularly Great Britain and the Netherlands to make substantial concessions because these countries were preoccupied with their own war effort made necessary by Nazi aggression in Europe. But nothing of the sort happened. On the contrary, rather than being divisive, Japanese military threats further encouraged allied cooperation. On August 15, 1941, for instance, the Dutch government-in-exile decided that it would declare war on Japan in the event of a Japanese attack on the United States or Great Britain. Partly also to protect the Dutch East Indies, the mighty British battleships *Prince of Wales* and *Repulse* arrived off Singapore's coast on December 1, 1941. Malacca, Singapore and the Indies felt safe again for a while. Not for long, however. A few days later, in the early morning of Sunday, December 7, the American naval base at Pearl Harbor in Hawaii woke up to a massive and merciless Japanese aerial attack. With one stroke, a substantial part of the American fleet was destroyed.

This memorable December 7 is to be regarded as the beginning of World War II in the Pacific. On that day not just the ships in Pearl Harbor went up in flames. On December 7, 1941, Japanese bombs also fell on Hong Kong and Manilla. And on that same fateful day, one and a half hours before the attack on Pearl Harbor, the Japanese landed near Kota Baru on the northern coast of Malacca, now Malaysia. The official Japanese declaration of war with the United States and Great Britain didn't come until the next day, on December 8. By then, the Dutch East Indies already were at war because on the day of the Pearl Harbor attack, the Dutch government had unilaterally declared war on Japan.

During the following days and weeks, Japan opened a large-scale offensive on various fronts. The first great blow came

December 10, when the *Prince of Wales* and the *Repulse*, both considered unsinkable, were destroyed near Singapore. On December 16, the Japanese landed on British Borneo, occupying Miri. Five days later, Japan and Siam, now Thailand, entered into an alliance, and Japanese troops landed on the important island of Luzon in the Philippines. And on December 25, the British surrendered Hong Kong. By the end of the month, in a final, desperate effort to stop the Japanese assault, American president Franklin D. Roosevelt and British prime minister Winston Churchill decided to create a united allied military command, the so-called ABDA Command, consisting of American, British, Dutch and Australian forces. On January 3, 1942, the day after Manilla surrendered, General Archibald P. Wavell, a laconic Scot, was appointed ABDA's supreme commander. In the middle of January, he made his headquarters in the town of Lembang on Java, Dutch East Indies. From then on, thousands of American and British infantry and air force personnel headed to the region, especially Java. The Australians were assigned to defend the Moluccas.

By then, on January 11, 1942, the Japanese also had entered the Dutch East Indies. The oil-rich island of Borneo, now called Kalimantan, was the first strategic target of Japan, which lacked substantial natural resources. Next, in rapid succession, the islands of Celebes – now called Sulawesi – Ambon, Bali and Timor were occupied.

Despite its planes and war ships, the ABDA Command could not stop the Japanese assault. On February 15, even Singapore as well as Palembang on Sumatra fell into Japanese hands: 130,000 British, Indian, Australian and local Malaysian and Singaporean soldiers became POWs. To be sure, six days later, General Wavell received urgent orders from Washington to defend Java to the bitter end, but by then the supreme commander had lost faith in his mission. After all, great parts of the Dutch Indies were already in Japanese hands. On February 25, the ABDA Command was dissolved, and Wavell flew back to the safety of Ceylon, now Sri Lanka. Two days later, the war at sea was also decided in the Java Sea when the Japanese destroyed the combined allied fleet that went by the proud name "Striking Force."

This left Java, the principal island of the Indies, wide open to an invasion. In the early morning of Sunday, March 1, 1942, 56 transport ships put ashore a Japanese force of 55,000 soldiers in four different places on Java's northern coast. In some places a fierce battle took place between the Japanese army and the Royal Netherlands East Indies Army (KNIL), but Japanese supremacy was far too great. A week later, H. ter Poorten, lieutenant-general of the KNIL, who had remained air force and army commander on Java under Wavell's ABDA Command, was forced to surrender unconditionally.

In April and May, the Japanese occupied Sumatra, New Guinea (now called Papua), and a number of smaller islands in the archipelago. Enlisted KNIL soldiers and draftees became POWs, some 68,000 overall. British, Australian and American soldiers who had been unable to escape after their brief ABDA adventure were detained and sent to POW camps. About 100,000 European and Indo-European women and children, boys under the age of seventeen, and men over 60 were interned in camps for civilians. Some civilians were interned immediately following the Japanese occupation; others, particularly on Java, were not incarcerated until the middle of 1943.

Indonesians and the majority of the Indo-European civilians designated as Asians by the Japanese remained outside the internment camps. This didn't mean, however, that their lives became any easier or safer. Despite the slogan "Asia for the Asians," the Japanese masters didn't have much good in store for them, either. Everywhere in the occupied territories, Indonesian men and women were recruited for the Japanese war effort, usually under false pretenses. Later on, many of them were simply taken off the streets or out of movie theaters and put to work as romushas. Women were forced into prostitution, a tragic fate that has been brought to our attention increasingly in the past several decades by the women themselves. Interest in the fate of the romushas also has increased. Japanese historians have shown that during the final year and a half of the Japanese occupation, about ten million Indonesian men, most of them Javanese, were forced to work in the military infrastructure, in industry and in agriculture. This recruitment of romushas eventually resulted in totally destabilizing Indonesian society. With not enough strong men left to work the land, food production collapsed, resulting in famine and many deaths.

Between Japan's invasion of Manchuria in 1931 and the end of World War II in 1945, tens of millions of people in South and Southeast Asia and the Pacific area died as a result of war. Even so, there still was no peace following the Japanese surrender on August 15, 1945. As early as August 17, Indonesian independence leaders Sukarno and Hatta proclaimed an independent

Republik Indonesia. The Dutch government was unmoved, and war followed upon war. This time, a free Indonesia was at stake. The country was no longer to be a colony of the Netherlands but a free country governed by Indonesians rather than Europeans. In addition to fresh troops from the Netherlands, the Dutch used former POWs freed from Japanese camps to fight the new republic, efforts that culminated in the so-called "police actions" of July 1947 and December 1948. And so Europeans and Indo-Europeans on the one hand and, on the other, Indonesian romushas, who all had shared a miserable fate on the railroads, ended up facing each other, weapons in hand, during Indonesia's war of independence.

The purpose of the Burma railroad was to link the existing Singapore-Bangkok-Saigon railway with the Ye-Moulmein-Pegu-Rangoon railway. The Japanese plan was to secure a supply line to the northern Burmese front, close to the border with India. The planned railway from Siam to Burma was to have a total length of 260 miles. The point of departure was the town of Nom Pladuk in Siam, where the new railway line connected with the line to Bangkok. The end of the new line was the town of Thanbyuzayat in Burma, which connected with the Moulmein-Ye line.

Tracing the Burma Railway's trajectory began in July 1942. The colossal project of building the railway was done by some 12,000 Japanese military railway personnel, more than 160,000 Asian romushas from Indonesia, Malacca, Burma, Siam and Singapore, and by close to 61,000 allied POWs. The latter consisted of nearly 28,600 British, nearly 20,000 Dutch, 12,000 Australian, and several hundred American men. Among the romushas from Malacca were many Tamils, whose ancestors had been taken by the British from southern India to work as indentured laborers on the Malacca plantations. The number of Japanese troops also included the mostly Korean guards. Their country had been annexed in 1910 by Japan and brutally colonized ever since. The relationship between the Japanese masters and their Korean servants was on the whole extremely bad. That didn't mean things were any better between the Koreans and railway workers. When allied prisoners complained to Japanese officers about their treatment by the Korean guards, the Koreans often took out their frustration on the defenseless prisoners.

Work on the railway was done from both ends at once, from Burma in the north and Siam in the South, working toward the middle. The prisoners building the north-south line came from Singapore by sea. Those working on the southern end went up by train from Singapore via Bangkok, a trip lasting four to five days. These transports were terrible. Many prisoners were undernourished and weakened by disease, and scores died *en route* to the railway sites. At the sites, the prisoners and romushas were forced to perform extremely hard labor using poor equipment with not nearly enough to eat. Four million cubic feet of earth had to be moved, three million cubic feet of rock had to be crushed, and bridges totaling almost nine miles in length had to be constructed.

About 190 miles of the Burma Railway ran through a virtually uninhabited tropical rain forest. Seven base camps served the entire track. The actual work camps lay alongside the track. These were little more than jungle clearings with some tents, barracks, a primitive kitchen and a few latrines. Sometimes, the prisoners and romushas were forced to work for more than 16 hours a day under a burning sun or in torrential monsoon downpours.

The Burma Railway was completed on October 17, 1943. The death toll was staggering: "A human life for every two sleepers" is a frequently heard expression in this context. Of the nearly 61.000 allied prisoners of war, almost one fourth died of abuse, exhaustion and tropical disease. That amounts to around 14,500 dead, of which about 8,500 were British, about 3,100 Dutch, around 2,650 Australian and around 130 American. The death rate among the 160,000 to 200,000 romushas is roughly estimated to have been around 50 percent, between 80,000 and 100,000 casualties. More exact numbers are not available.

The principal reason for constructing the Sumatra railroad was the transport of military material and troops right through the Sumatran interior. The 140 miles of railway between Pekanbaru and Muaro would thus be the missing link between East and West Sumatra. The railway was also meant to transport coal, of which there was plenty in Sumatra.

As early as April 1943, Javanese romushas began constructing the bank for this railroad. Well over a year later, in May of 1944, the first gang of POWs arrived in Pekanbaru. In the end, they would total 4,967: 3,886 Dutchmen, 1,065 Englishmen and Australians, 15 Americans, and one Norwegian sailor whose ship had been torpedoed. The army of romushas who worked on the railroad, initially Javanese but later joined by Sumatrans, gradually increased to an estimated 98,000. Transport ships crowded with POWs and romushas supplied nearly all of these future railroad workers. British submarines twice accidentally torpedoed such a slave ship because the British commanders thought the ships carried Japanese war equipment rather than their own people. The most tragic instance was the sinking of the Junyo Maru on September 18, 1944, off the western coast of Sumatra, one of the greatest shipping disasters in history. There were around 6,500 men on board, among them more than 4,200 romushas from Java. At least 5,620 of those on board drowned.

Thirteen camps were constructed between Pekanbaru and Muaro. Many young and strong POWs had already been sent to work in Burma or Siam. Those toiling at the Sumatra Railway were relatively older and weaker men. Even so, the workers were still forced to work 10 hours a day on average in miserable conditions. In the final weeks before completion, gangs worked for 36 hours non-stop with just two or three hours rest. Ironically, the Sumatra Railway was finished on August 15, 1945, the day Japan surrendered. During construction about 76,000 Indonesian romushas and nearly 700 POWs died of hunger and disease. This does not include the victims of the allied torpedo attacks. After September 1945, the Sumatra Railway was never used again. Transporting a few trainloads of coal and returning the railway slaves were, therefore, the only functions the railroad ever had. The romushas were at first simply abandoned, roaming the countryside for months, hungry and stealing food, which caused great anger among the local population.

Up until just a few years ago, little was known in England, the Netherlands, and Australia about the romushas, and in America nothing whatsoever. Whatever interest the western world had in the War in the Pacific was almost exclusively focused on POWs of European descent. The worldwide success of the 1957 movie *The Bridge on the River Kwai* contributed to this. The movie received seven Oscars but didn't feature a single Indo-European or romusha.

Incidentally, the POWs were not an ethnically homogeneous group. This group consisted, after all, of full-blooded European and Indo-European POWs. Even though the latter officially belonged to the European segment of the population in the pre-war East Indies, they still took a back seat in the colonial hierarchy because of the color of their skin. At the same time, the colonial hierarchy demanded that Indo-Europeans keep a certain distance from the full-blooded Indonesians. During the Japanese occupation, things changed dramatically indeed. The Dutch had been beaten after a brief fight by the Japanese, whom they considered inferior. Subsequently the colonial system was completely dismantled. From then on, the Japanese ruled the roost. The Indonesians came second, and the Indo-Europeans and Europeans were relegated to the bottom of the hierarchy.

If at all possible, the distance between Europeans and Indonesians became greater still in the camps along the railway lines. The Japanese kept the POWs and the romushas fully segregated in most camps. In some camps POWs were even forbidden to make any contact with romushas. This happened anyway, of course, if only to barter for food.

The death toll of both railways is simply horrifying. The great difference in the number of dead between romushas and POWs triggers questions about their living conditions and treatment by the Japanese. It's obviously a fact that the Asians and a great many of the Indo-Europeans were better adapted to the climate and to other local conditions. This is also partially confirmed in the accounts by some of the people interviewed for this book. The Asians knew better than the Europeans where to find edible plants and how to make use of medicinal herbs found in the jungle for treating diseases and tropical sores. They were at home there, knew how to find paths and animal tracks, and they were better hunters. And having better food to eat under those terrible conditions along the railway lines meant a better chance of surviving.

On the other hand, the romushas had to perform the heaviest work on the railway, there was hardly any medical aid for them, and they got even less to eat than the POWs. Perhaps even more detrimental to the romushas was the absence of a sound organization with people in charge. Even during their captivity, the POWs were still under the command of their own officers, who did not have to perform heavy physical labor, at least not on Sumatra. Military hierarchy, discipline and routine gave structure to the lives of the POWs. And such a structure increased the chance of survival. Compared to this, the romushas were little more than "a rag-tag band," as POW Frans Banning says in this book. Indonesia has a great many different ethnic groups, and the romushas had been recruited or rounded up in widely different parts of the country and thrown together by the Japanese without any regard for ethnicity. Moreover, not just Indonesian romushas worked on the Burma Railway, but also forced laborers from Malacca, Singapore, Burma and Thailand, most of whom didn't even speak the same language. The POWs, on the other hand, mostly worked in small groups, so-called *kongis*, and they helped one another. The romushas were, however, without mutual support because they lacked social and hierarchical structure and ethnic ties. The result was an extremely high death rate. The Japanese didn't care one way or another. They found it simpler and more efficient to bring on fresh supplies of romushas than to spend energy and resources on the sick.

It is clear from these interviews, by the way, that the romushas were more likely to try an escape. That was nothing strange, since they could easily blend in with the local population. Europeans, on the contrary, had no effective chance of escaping because their western appearance would inevitably give them away.

Indonesian historical accounts have done little to highlight the fate of the romushas. In all of Indonesia there are just a few small monuments honoring the memory of the romushas. The small, concrete column erected just after the war on the cemetery of Camp 2 of the Sumatra Railway disappeared within a year by Japanese request. Director S. A. Karim's 1973 Indonesian movie *Romusha*, depicting their ordeal, was not distributed in Indonesia. The department of censorship of the Indonesian Ministry of Information probably prohibited its release under pressure from the Japanese embassy in Jakarta. The movie might have been perceived as harmful to economic relationships with Japan.

Probably even more important than trade with Japan is in this regard the Indonesian revolution. Following the surrender of Japan, the new *Republik Indonesia* was too preoccupied with its struggle for independence to worry about the romushas. The still uncertain future was simply more important than the past, no matter how bitter. This eminently suited president Sukarno, by the way, for he had been involved in the recruitment of romushas. To be sure, after the war Sukarno acknowledged that the Japanese regime had inflicted great misery and that he himself shared a responsibility for the sad fate of the romushas. He nonetheless washed his hands of the episode by arguing that, after all, a war of independence required sacrifices. And independence only could have been secured with the support of the Japanese.

Regardless of the politics during and immediately after World War II, every former forced laborer, whether brown-skinned or white-skinned, has to live with his very personal memories. The 24 men who tell their story in this book conjure up striking, moving, improbable and painful images. Their experiences are etched in their aged bodies. These are small monuments, not made of stone, but of images and words filled with emotion.

Authors

Dr. Esther Captain (b. 1969) is a historian and co-director of Het Indisch Huis in The Hague, a cultural and historical center dedicated to World War II in the former Dutch East Indies. In 2002, she received her Ph.D. from Utrecht University in the Netherlands; her dissertation is *Achter het kawat was Nederland* ("Behind the Fence Was the Netherlands"), Kampen, 2002, an analysis of journals and memoirs by civilian internees in Japanese prison camps. She is the author of several books and articles on memories of the war in the Indies and third-generation Indo-Europeans in the Netherlands. A number of her articles have been translated into English and Bahasa Indonesia.

Henk Hovinga (b. 1931) is a journalist and author whose specialty is Indonesia and the history of World War II in the Pacific. He has written numerous articles about these subjects and produced dozens of radio broadcasts and several television documentaries. His best-known book is the standard work *Eindstation Pakan Baroe 1943-1945,* 4th ed., Amsterdam, 1996. It has been translated into English as *Final Destination Pakan Baroe* and is available on CD-rom from the author: <henk.hovinga@tiscali.nl>.

24 Portraits

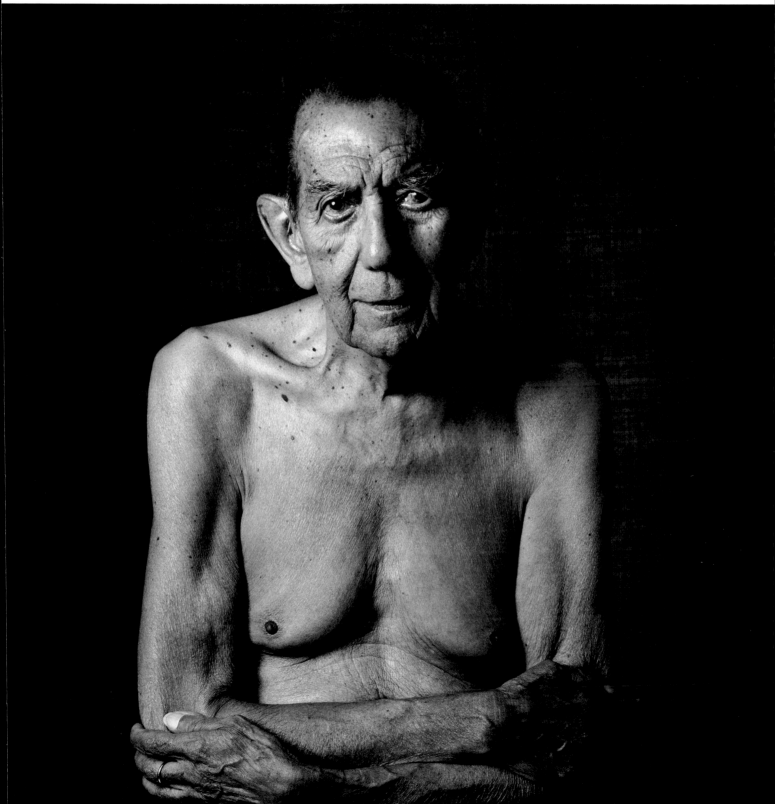

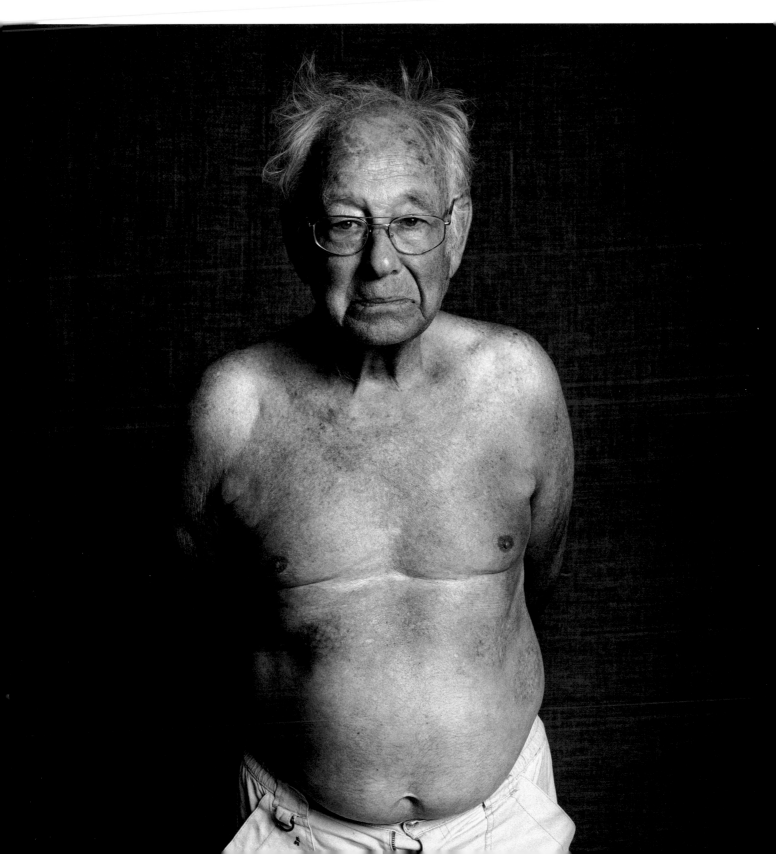

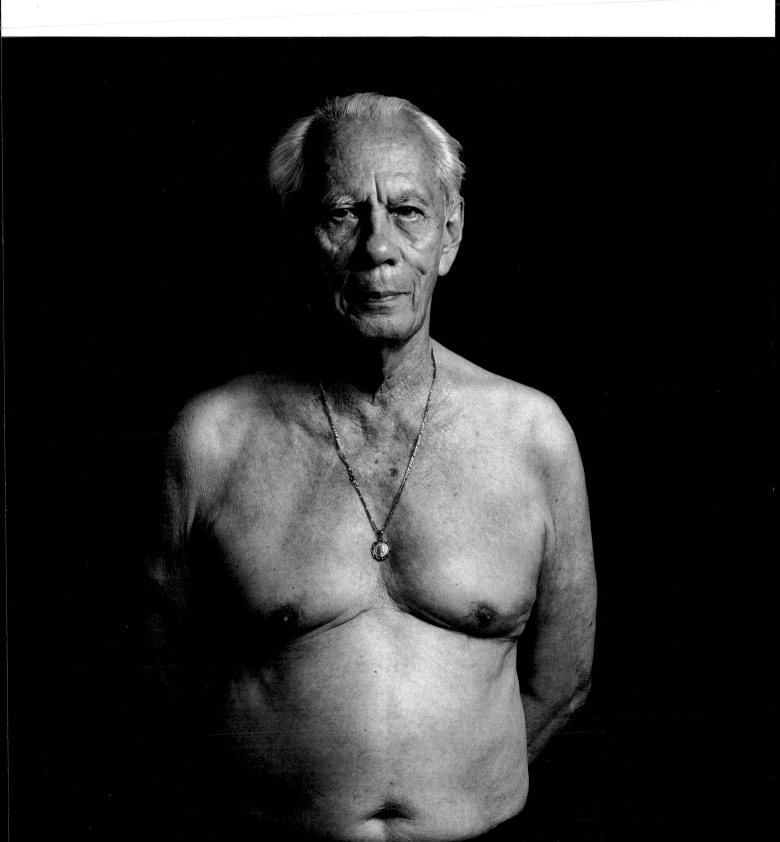

30 > 81   Han de Bruïne

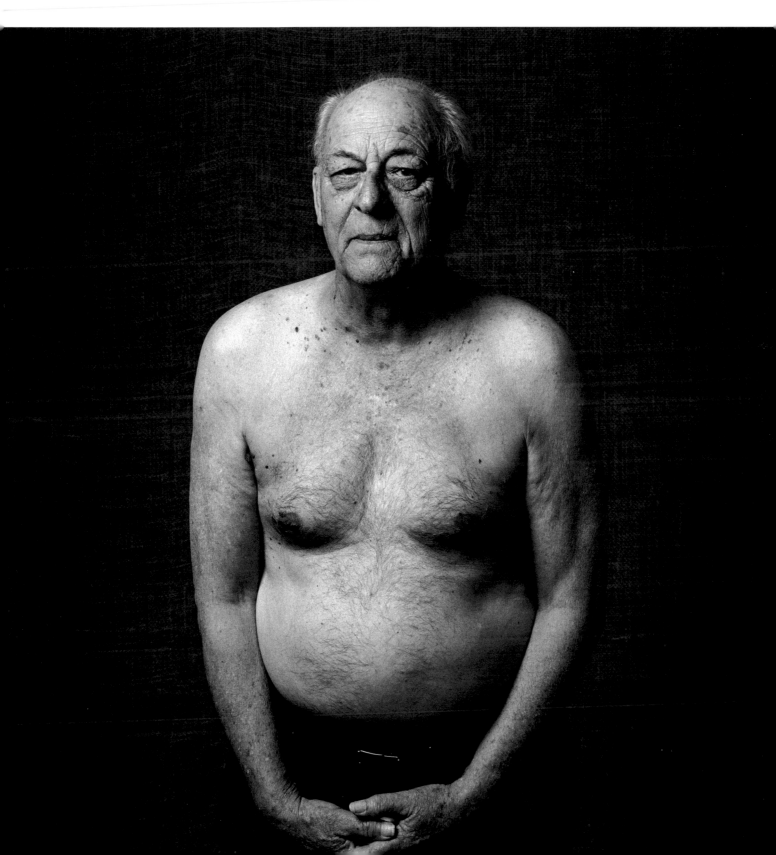

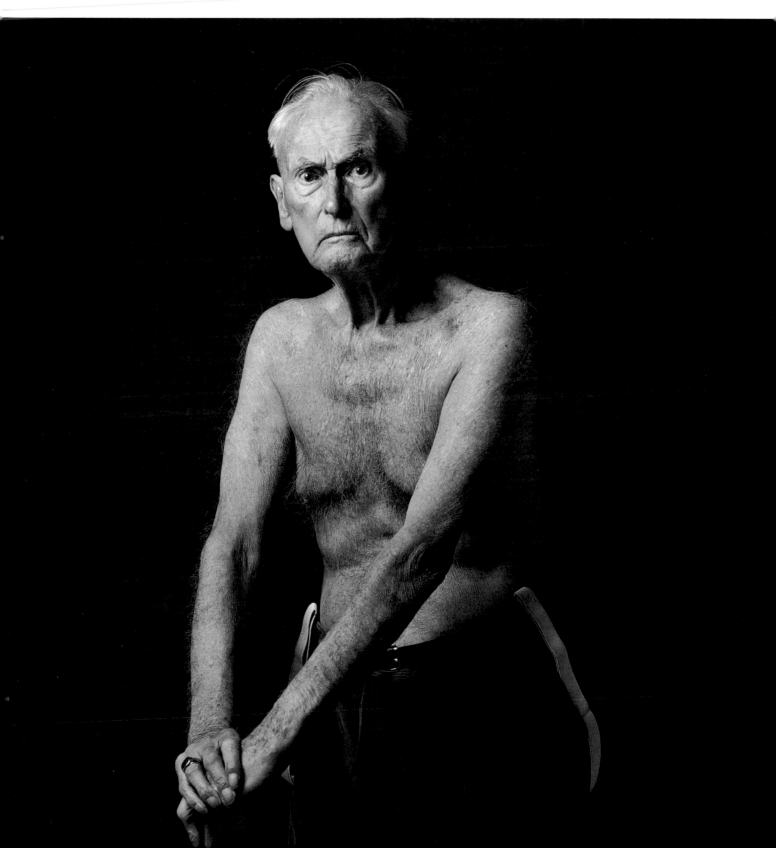

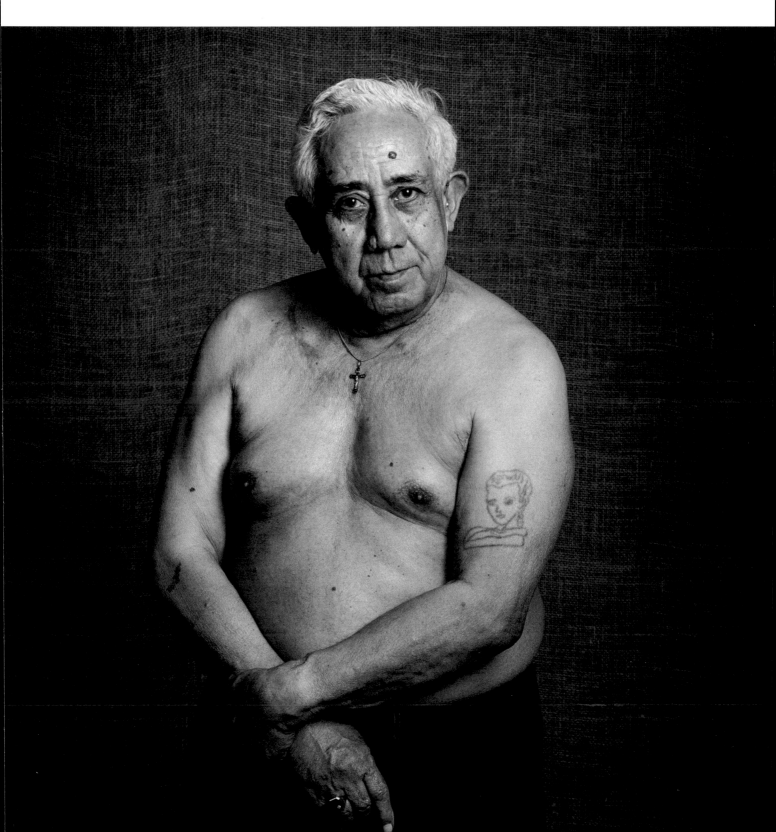

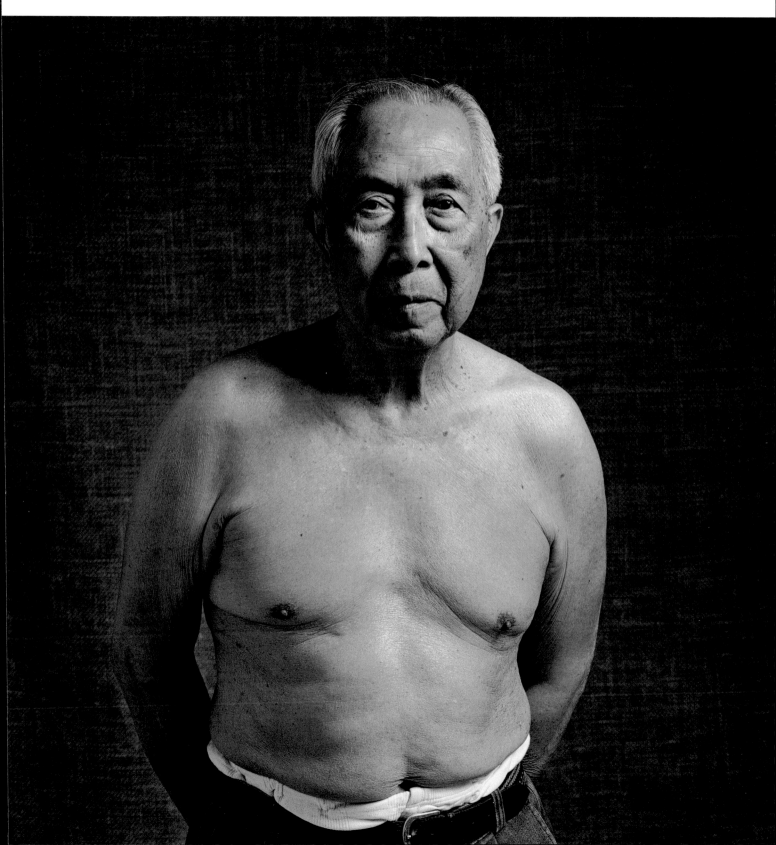

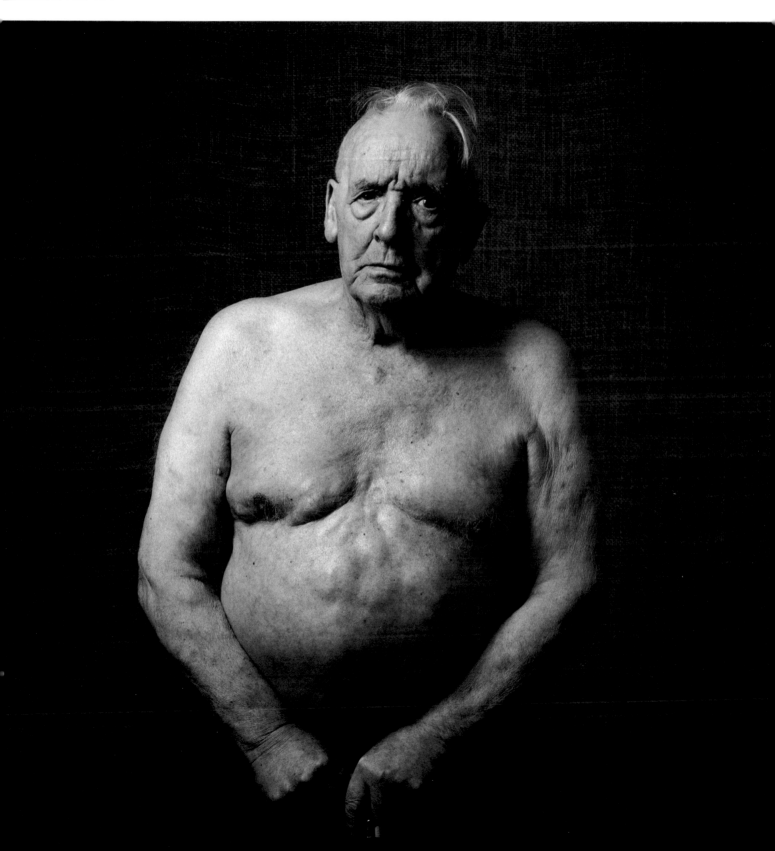

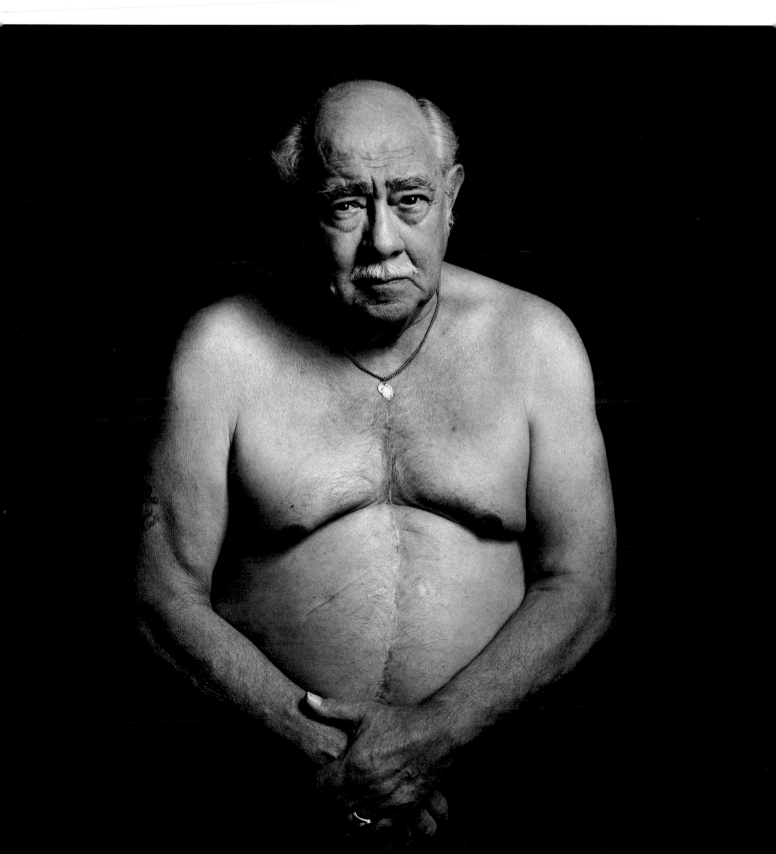

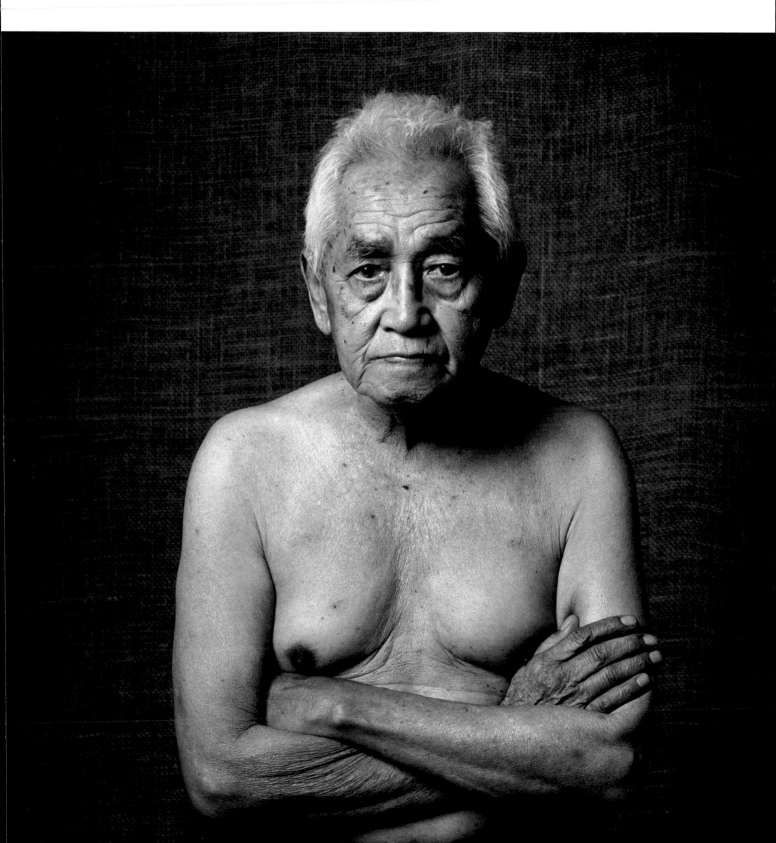

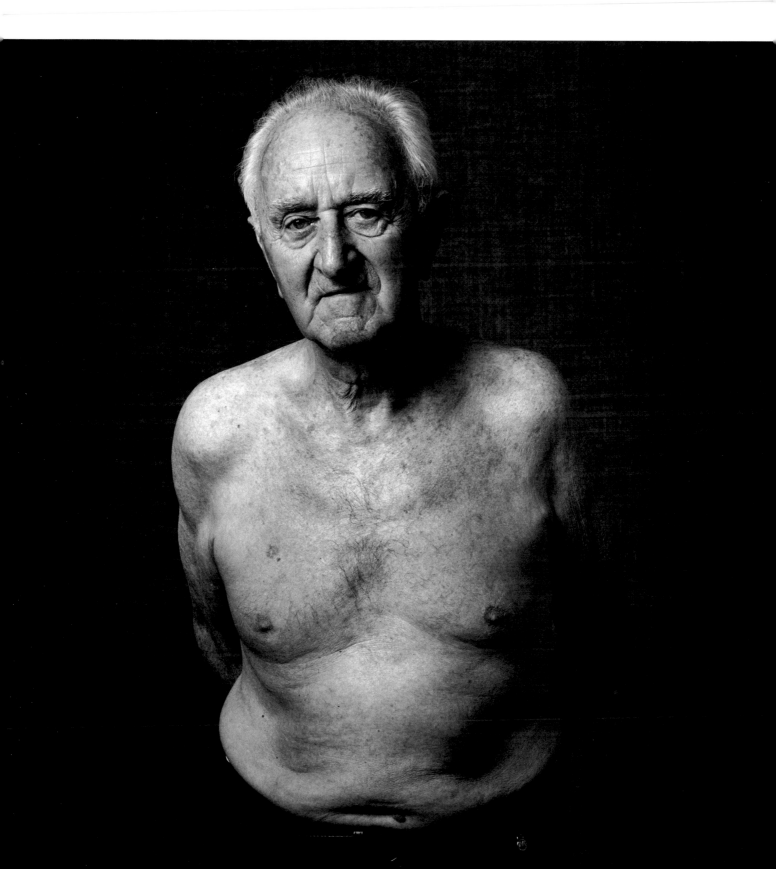

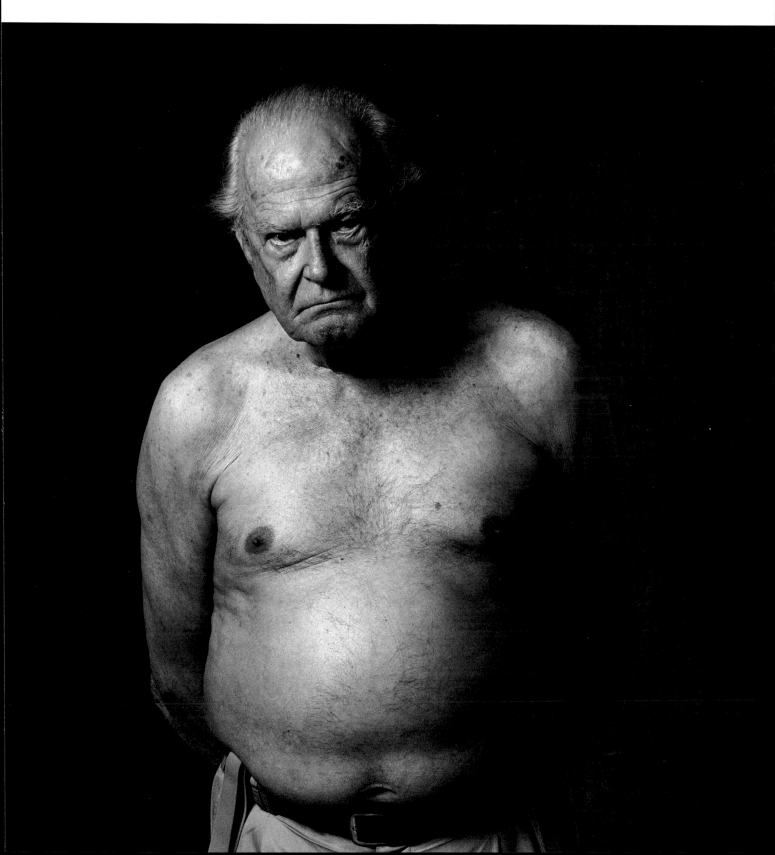

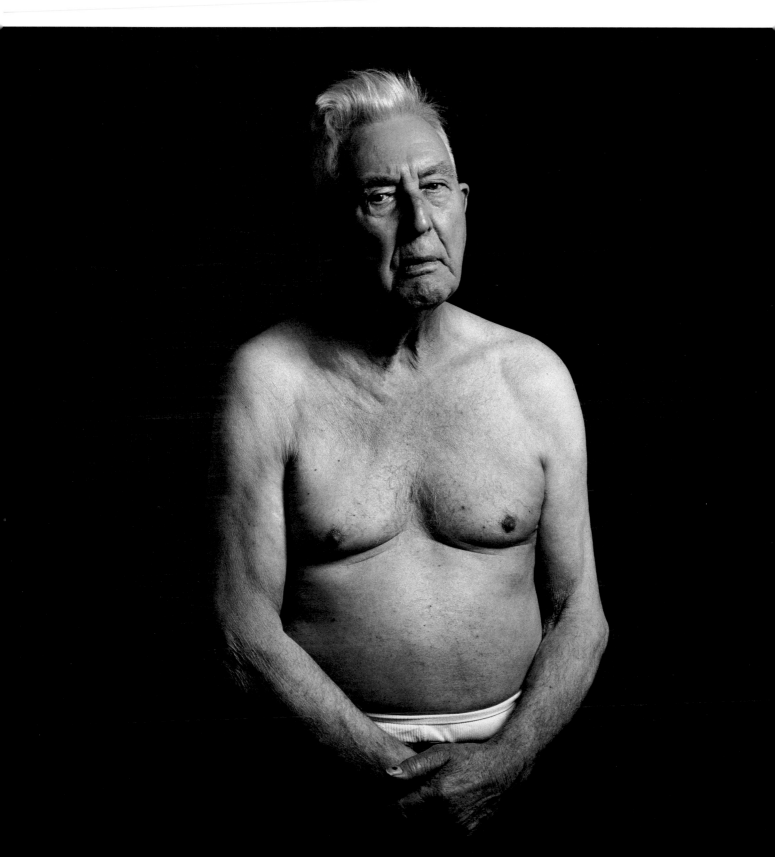

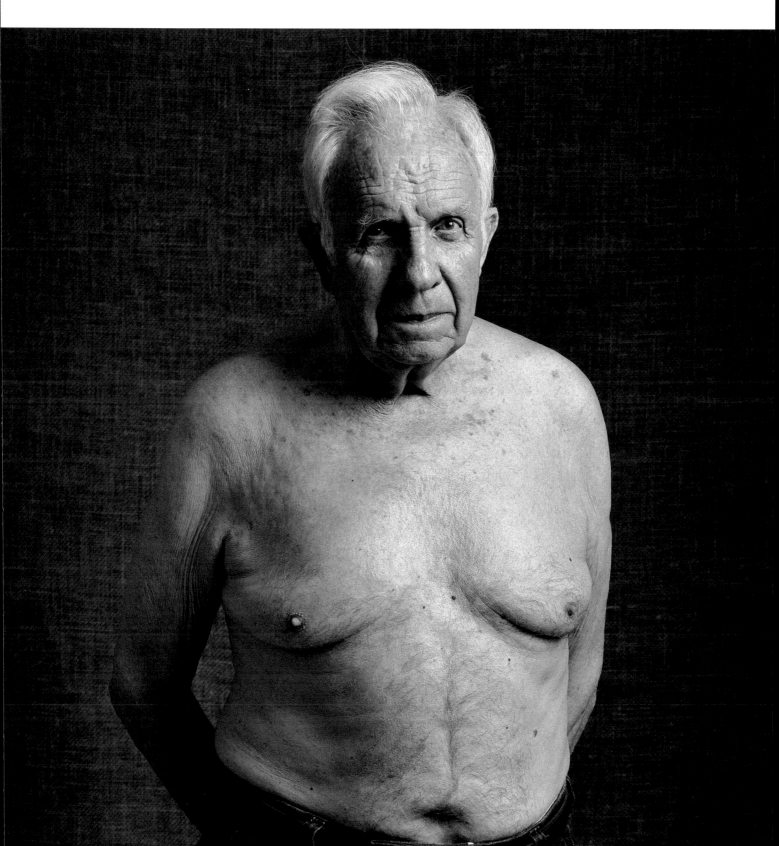

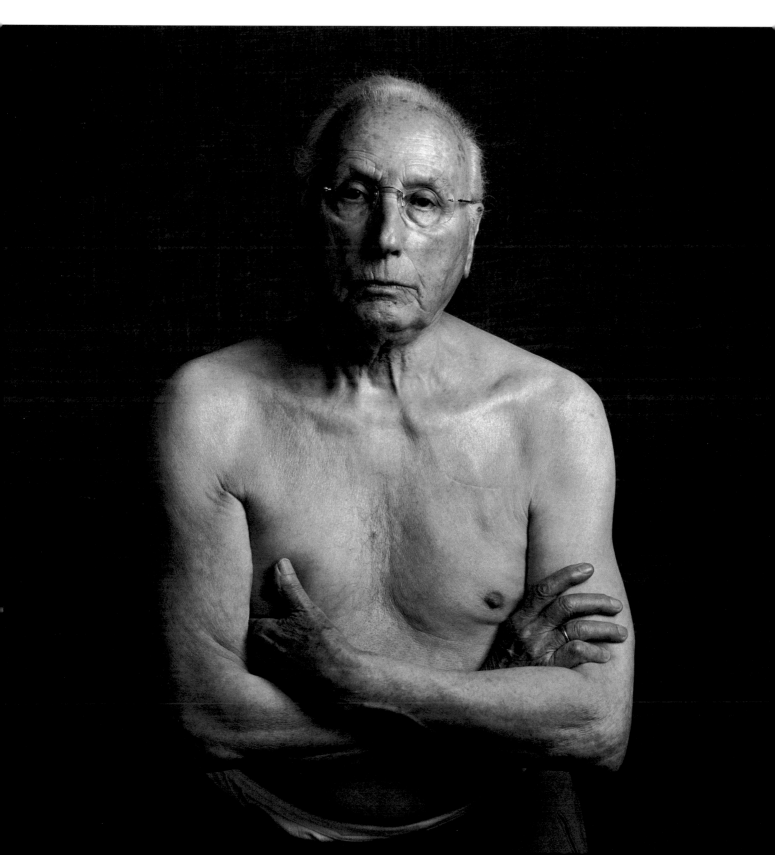

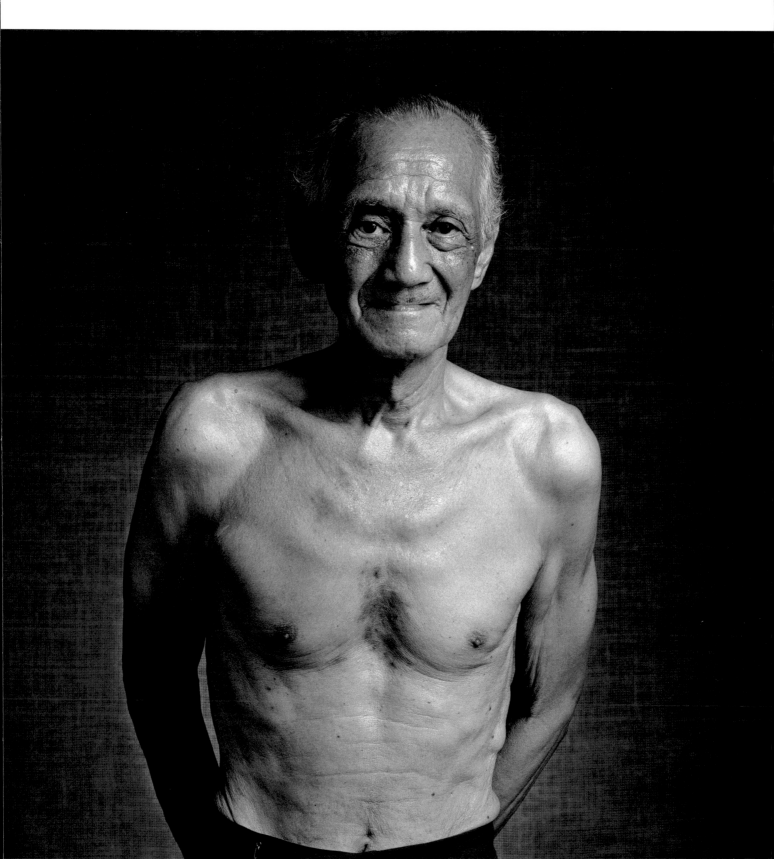

56 > 117   Damin

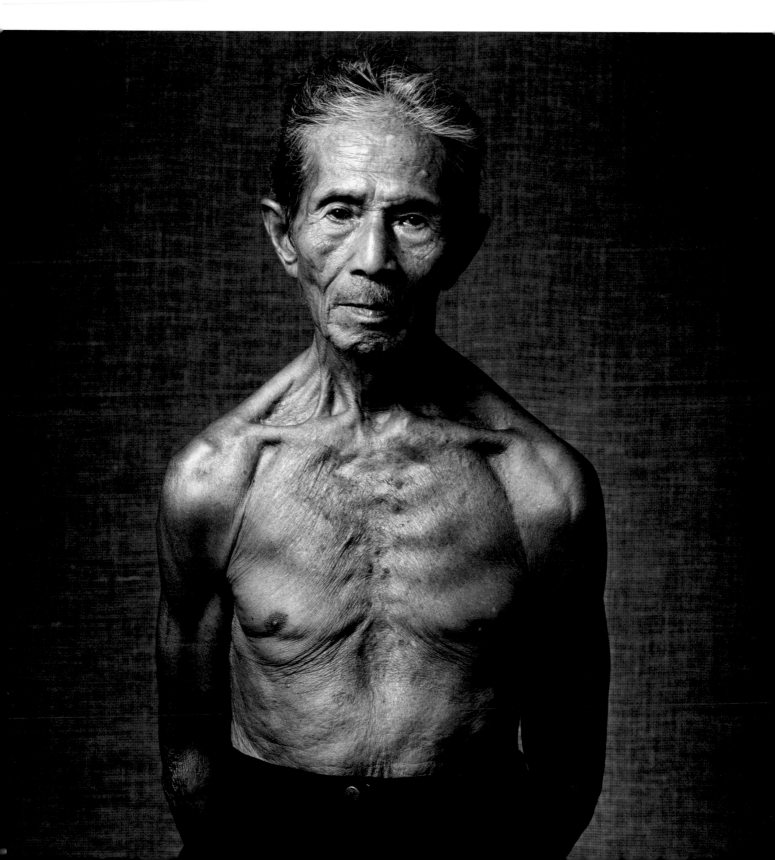

58 > 119   Dulrahman (Sidul)

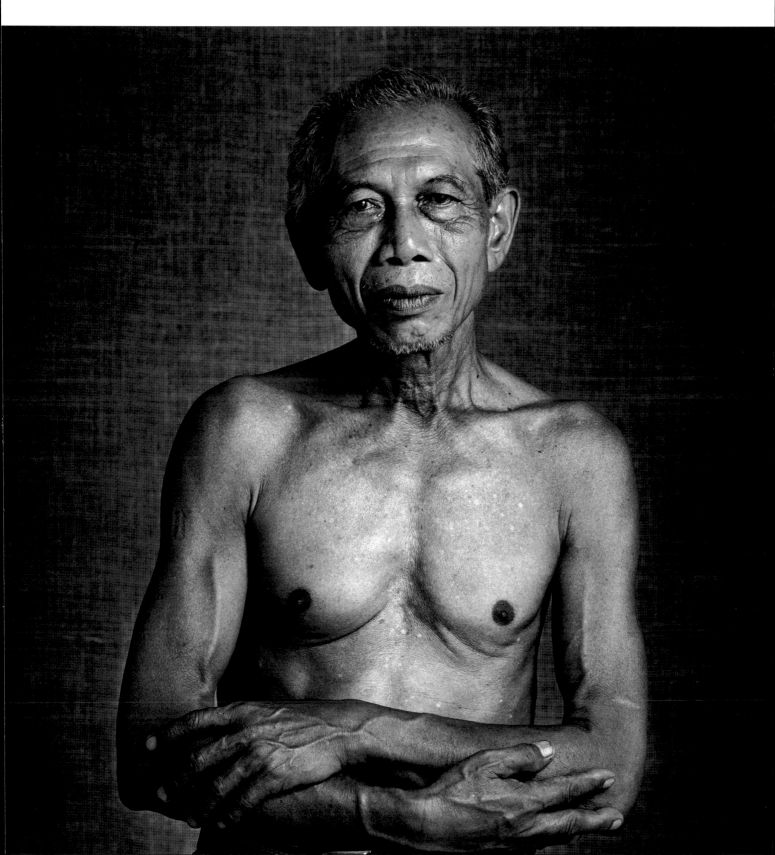

60 > 122   Ngadari

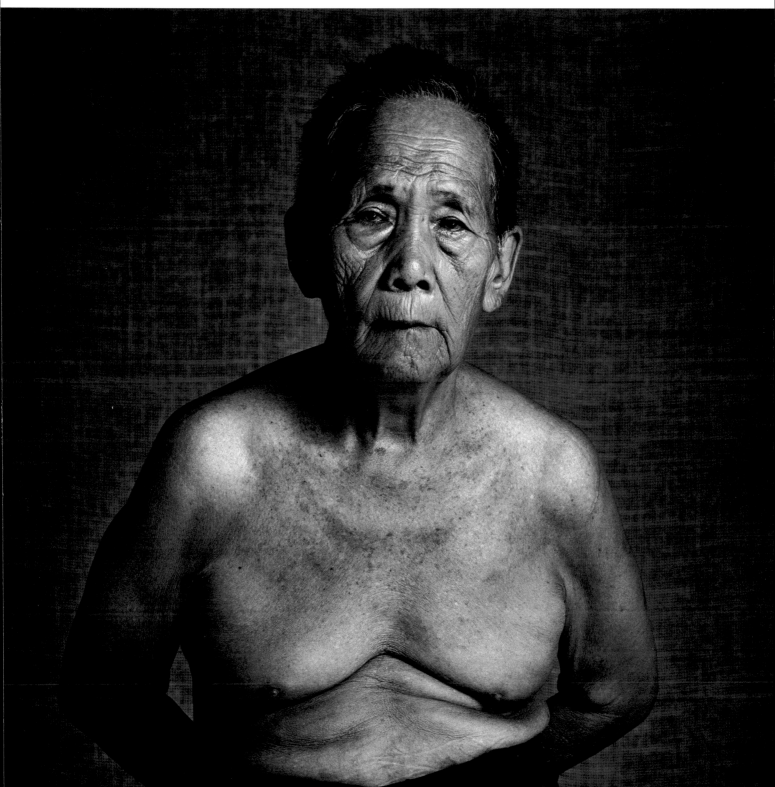

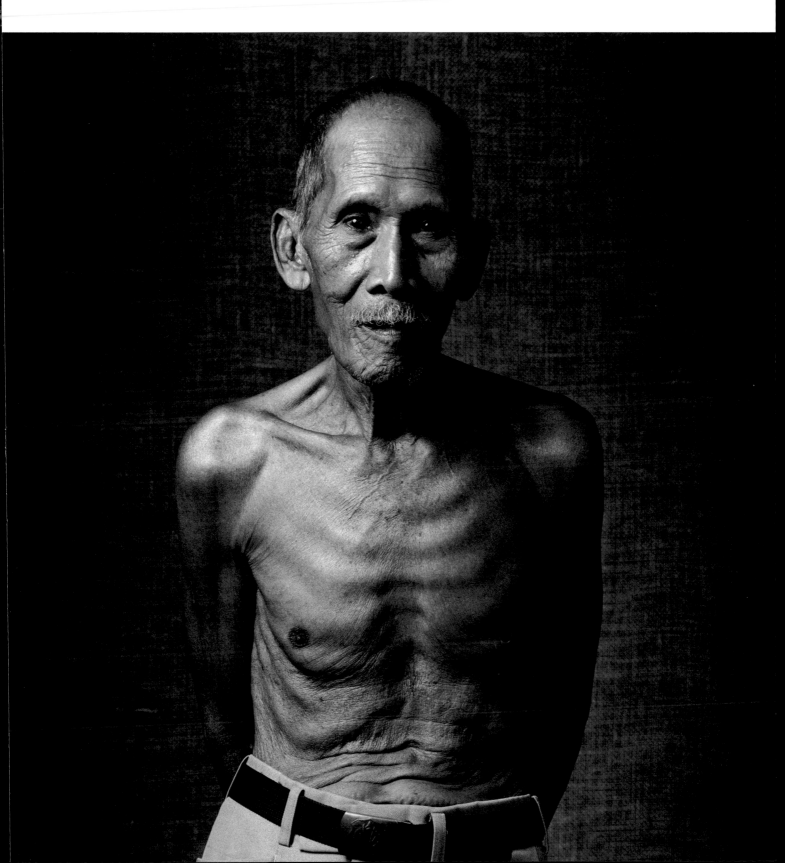

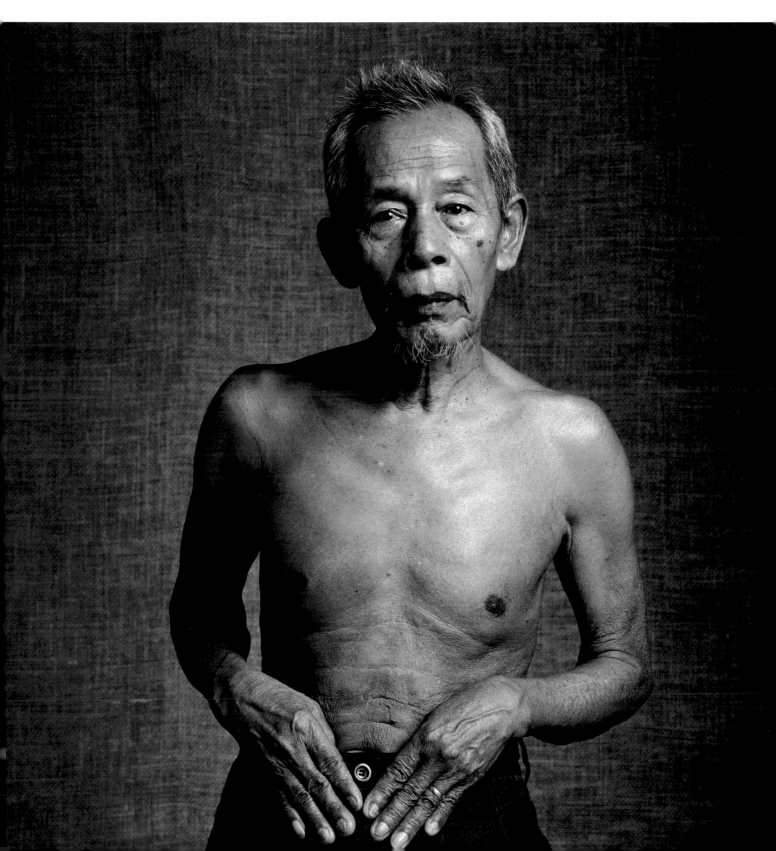

68 > 131 Sardi

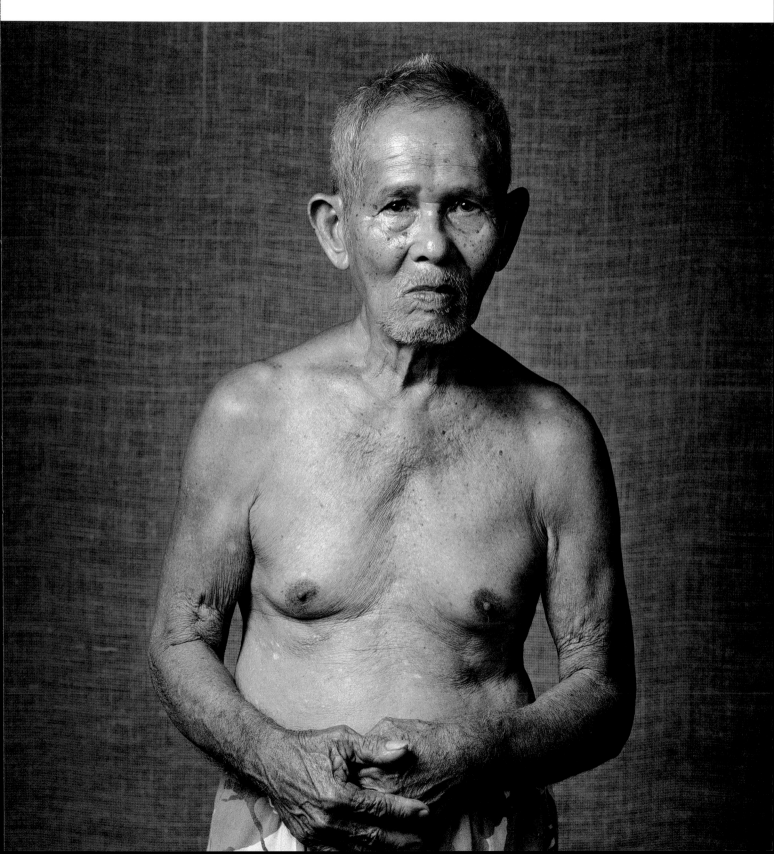

Jos van Arcken

"I really should have been dead long ago."

Born August 16, 1910, in Batavia, now Jakarta.
Volunteered as a soldier in the colonial army. As
a POW, he was forced to work for the Japanese
on the Sumatra Railway. His profession before and
after the war was that of watchmaker, first until
1958 in Jakarta, after that in the Netherlands.

"They shipped me out to Pekanbaru in May 1944.
The time on board was pure misery. Then a truck
took us from Pajakumbu to Pekanbaru. Halfway
across Sumatra we saw the Bukit Barisan, very much
like the Grand Canyon in America, only all of it
is covered in green. But it was so extraordinarily
beautiful that everybody on that truck got all
excited about nature's beauty. Its very splendor
made you forget all your troubles. Someone called
out: 'Before you know it, I'll start writing a book
entitled *My Travels with Nippon*.

In Pekanbaru itself, we found a meadow with
ditches along the Siak River, but there were no barracks to be seen, nothing at all. As it turned out,
we were the ones to build them. Soon thereafter, we
were put to work building the railroad. Some of that
came, of course, with a beating or two. We proved
a little work shy at first, and the moment the Jap
got wind of our disinclination, he started to let us
have it. I ended up in camp number 2, which ulti-
mately became our sickbay. That's where I actually
spent the remainder of the war. I got this tropical
ulcer. And if anything was the matter with you,
you saw to it that you didn't get better too fast.
So the moment the ulcer started to heal, you began
to neglect it. That wound was the thing that saved
your skin for it kept you away from that railroad.
I was still able, however, to walk through our com-
pound to go and fix watches

It was my good luck to be a professional
watchmaker, for the Japanese were crazy to a man
about watches. As luck would have it, I had a small

tool kit on me. All the Japanese knew about that,
and they would come to me to have their watch
fixed. I repaired them to the best of my ability.
In return, they'd give me salted fish, green peas
and sugar, in short, all kinds of stuff I could
certainly use very well.

There came a time when we had 11 dead per
day. Normally, we had five or six, but as the war
wore on, increasingly more people kicked the bucket
because of the poor food and the lack of medicine.
I, too, got sick with malaria and dysentery. That
dysentery was so destructive that I saw my own
end drawing near. If you had that, you didn't last
long. Most of us didn't survive beyond five or six
days. However, I was thinking, why not ask the
Japanese, for I happened to know quite a few of
them, and they knew me. So I went and asked the
male nurse in our sickbay, would he be willing to
go to the Japanese office and tell them: The watchmaker – let me see, the word in Japanese... there,
I have it again, the *tokeija* – is *bioki*, is sick, he's
got dysentery and he'd like to have some medicine.
And that very same day I got a handful of pills,
and those saved me. There were 12 of us in one
barracks and of those 12 just me and one other
guy survived. Because I had repaired their watches,
I got medicine. That's why I think my profession,
that of being a watchmaker, is an ideal profession.

I still think about what happened in the
war a lot. Quite a lot. And I also talk about it a
great deal. I know people who say: 'The war, that's
ancient history, I don't care to talk about that any
more.' However, I tend to think that those people
are not quite all there, mentally, I mean. If you
refuse to talk about the war, then...

I don't talk about it to young people born
after the war. But the moment I run into strangers
my own age or a bit younger, I begin to talk about
those days: Where were you, what about the conditions in your camp, the food, the beatings – sad
stuff, on the whole, because nice things are in
short supply during a war. Just sad stuff.

The thing I think about a lot is this: In those days, the thing we missed more than anything was freedom. Now we are free. And time and again I begin to make comparisons, for example about the food. Whenever I don't quite enjoy what I'm eating, I try to think back and remember how things tasted during the war. Or take being in pain, when you're sick, for example. We do feel pain once in a while, although toothaches are a thing of the past for me, but there's still pain in your knees, or in your back, for example. Whatever the pain I experience now, it's nothing compared to the pain I felt then. Sometime during the war, a Jap hit me with the butt of his rifle. About 10 years ago, they happened to make an X ray of my back, and one vertebra wasn't normal. That hit with the Jap's rifle had been hard enough to cause me to feel pain even today, particularly when I'm lying in bed. I still feel that to this day.

Meanwhile, I've become blind in one eye, but that has nothing to do with the war, that's a cataract operation gone wrong. It's very possible that insufficient nourishment hasn't done my eyes any good. And now, of course, I'm a watchmaker by profession, and that requires me to have good eyesight, for watches are pretty small. And as to my hearing, that hasn't improved any either. My hearing also has gotten very bad, so now I walk around with a hearing aid. But for the rest, I can't complain. My blood pressure is up to par, the heart is ticking away nicely, and all that despite my 91 years. I've come to realize that I'm one of the lucky ones, because I really should have been dead long ago. I really feel lucky to be alive, that despite all my aches and pains I have reasons to be happy once in a while and tell some jokes."

Frans Banning

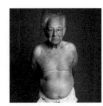

"It was over, and you didn't talk about it anymore."

Born April 5, 1921, in Makassar, on the Indonesian island of Sulawesi, then called Celebes. A draftee in the colonial army, he became a POW and in May 1944 was sent to work on the Sumatra Railway. After the war, he worked as a chemist in the textile industry.

"I've never worried about a thing. Being made a prisoner of war was just something I accepted and endured. All I thought was: We'll just have to see how we're going to get out of this one. But why worry about anything? During the final month of the war, fortunately just toward the end, when I got dysentery in addition to malaria, I ended up in the back of sickbay, in the very corner of those who'd been written off. There were six of us. A priest came to visit us. I said: 'Father, what are you doing here?' 'I've come to administer the holy sacrament of the dying.' 'But why? I'm not dying at all. Whatever gave you that idea?'

Of those six men, just one survived, and that was me. I've always felt justified in thinking that things would turn out alright. I've always been an optimist. Don't forget, odd as it seems, you were then in a state of mind where you allowed yourself to be lived, as it were. You simply accepted everything, though you helped one another whenever you could, you tried to avoid doing anything stupid, of course. Oh, is that what we are supposed to do? Well, fine, let's go to it and try to avoid making accidents.

Towards the end, well, sure, you just tried to survive, tried to get enough to eat, tried to keep others from stealing your stuff, but for the rest... Not having any prospects, that's what did you in. It's what dulled all of us. Every day was the same. We were without any news whatsoever about developments beyond our POW camp, beyond the Sumatra Railway. So you didn't know which way the war was going, either against us or in our favor. Will there never be an end to it all? You didn't see the big picture, just that stupid Sumatra Railway where you had to lay yet another rail the next day. That very lack of prospects was what killed the will to live in a lot of people. Because there were people who were sick and who totally lacked the will to live. Those died. Other people, actually written off by the doctor, managed to stay alive against all odds.

When we arrived in Holland, in April of 1946, my health was still a bit iffy, I think. They gave me a medical check and still found residual dysentery. But for the rest it didn't bother me, for me the war had ended. Gosh, you meet your Dutch family, your circumstances change entirely, circumstances you've never encountered before.

No, I can't say I have the impression that the Sumatra period has had a negative impact on me. A positive impact, perhaps, in that I have come to regard my fellow man in a different light. I'm more interested in the person himself than in his position. I am more inclined to speak my mind, less afraid to stand up and be counted. I'm not easily impressed anymore by people with a big mouth or by someone who announces: 'I'm the one who's in charge here!' Those days are over. I try to see through that sort of thing. But, of course, that's not just because of Sumatra, but also because of my stay, later on, in the United States.

I'm no longer as likely to allow someone else to change my mind or influence me. I'm the one who will decide if I can handle something or not. Naturally, you become a lot more levelheaded and you learn to think for yourself. Working on that railroad back then made you a lot more suspicious of others because people cheated you and stole your stuff. Perhaps I was too gullible and too optimistic where other people were concerned. I've since learned to keep my distance and to be careful what you tell others. I have not let that bother me since, though.

Army discipline totally governed our life in the POW camp, our work there and our relations to one another. That's what was tragically lacking among the *romushas*,[1] they had nothing of the kind, they lacked any form of discipline, lacked all cohesion, they were just a bunch of people thrown together. That's one thing the war taught us, every society needs order, needs some sort of authority, otherwise things become a total shambles. In our camp, the rule of law was very evident, and that turned out to be a blessing. If it hadn't been for that, the riffraff would have had a field day. You even had to be careful they didn't lift your eating bowl. I've concluded that if the situation is lousy, given half a chance, people will not hesitate to take advantage of one another. When conditions are lousy, there's no solidarity whatsoever. If you were not part of a so-called *kongsi*, a team made up of two or three men, then you were in for it, then you could be taken advantage of in every way imaginable.

Me throw out food? Not likely. No, you've got to clean your plate. Not because you paid good money for it, but, come on, throw it out? My goodness, in those days you would kill to get an extra morsel of food. And there would be hell to pay if you noticed that the next guy got a larger portion of food than you did. Any suspicion of unfairness would create mayhem. Sure, even to this day, if at all possible, I save a little something to eat for tomorrow. That's become second nature. The same goes for my idea of honesty and justice. And I very much need my privacy. Maybe that's a reason for not traveling or staying in groups, something my wife Wil didn't like, either.[2] Good gracious no, no groups, please, no more responding like a herd to what people tell you to do, that was just something we could not handle anymore. You always had to do

everything as a group, you stood forever in line to get food. There was this time when we were on holiday at a campground. Underneath a boiling hot sun, we found ourselves in a long line to get an ice cream cone. That's when it got to be too much for Wil and me both. My God, it was like being in camp all over again, having to stand in line to get food. No sir, no more camping, no more standing in line for us ever again, that was just too awful.

My father worked on the railroad as well, on the Burma Railway, apparently on the Thai side of the border. But I know absolutely nothing of his experiences of that time. We just never talked about it. My guess is we postponed the need to do so, maybe hid it, because both of us were very preoccupied. I was preoccupied with my family, my job, especially my job. As for him, his health wasn't great and that worried him a lot. The few times we met, which was mostly on weekends, the children would usually take up all of our time. Besides, in those days people never talked about the war at all. You talked about your job, about the kids, and, my goodness, to my everlasting shame and sorrow, I never had even one conversation with him about our common past. Simply too stupid for words. Yes, I neglected them, my parents, that's what it really comes down to.

On his deathbed, in 1970, he did refer to various things from before the war. But even then he never said a thing about having been a POW, and I then clearly did not have the urge, in haste, say, and before it was too late, to learn a thing or two about that period of his life. Apparently, neither of us felt the need then to talk about that. Dad was, for that matter, not very inclined to have contact with other people anyway, and I've never had the impression that, hey, Dad's been talking about his POW experiences, he has met so and so from those days. No, I sooner think that my father, and perhaps his entire generation, never took the trouble to even think about those experiences much. They repressed it, it was over and done with, and you

1 Along the Sumatra Railway, these Asian civilians, forced to work by the Japanese, were mainly from the island of Java.

2 She spent the war in Japanese civilian internment camps.

didn't talk about it. There was no point. But now it turns out that children and grandchildren very much would like to know more about that period in the life of their father or grandfather, and some of those oldsters are just not talking.

After I retired, we visited Indonesia a couple of times and we, Wil and I, we also got around to visiting the place on Sumatra where I worked on the railway. And then it became apparent that there clearly was a great psychological need to get to know more about that whole situation.

At first, there were never any leads or links, not until you came into contact with people who had experienced the same thing. Not until I finally had enough time, after my retirement, that is, I got around to becoming a member of those various societies, you name them, that concern themselves with that period of history. I don't recall there were very many conferences of that sort before the 1980s. That's really something that didn't take off until the last 10, 20 years or so. People are delighted about these opportunities, and, believe me, they all talk a lot about the past there.

That's when you get to think about it and read about it. I afterwards tried to get to know more about my father, but unfortunately I didn't really focus on his past until after his death. I started reading about the Sumatra and Burma Railways after my retirement. I think that more than anything else explains the fact that, first, I never discussed it with my father and, second, why for the longest time I never was much interested in my own affairs, either.

And if anything did happen to come by, then I could always talk about it with Wil. She sensed right away what was going on, she knew because she'd been in the war herself and knew a thing or two about the Japs. We had a very strong bond in that respect. Not that we talked about it a lot either, you know. Just having been in the Indies both of us created a strong bond. You didn't need to go into any particulars, you simply understood things. That meant that you could say 'Oh, yes, that,' and whenever you read a book you'd say, 'Wil, did you read that?' 'Yes, nice, isn't it?' That was enough. Then you knew right away what it was all about. Without ever saying a thing, there was a great deal you both had experienced, albeit under different circumstances. You didn't need to talk about that."

Alex Bloem

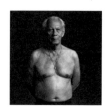

"When you come right down to it,
we're strangers here, you know."

Born May 6, 1921, in Bandung on the island of
Java. He was a professional soldier who was made
POW. In September 1944, he shipped out on the
Junyo Maru[1] to work on the Sumatra Railway.
The ship was torpedoed.
After the war, he was a noncommissioned officer
and later worked for an insurance bank.

"On the morning of September 15, 1944, we were
ordered to fall in line. We were then marched off
to Senen, the new station. On arriving in Tanjung
Priok,[2] we saw a lot of romushas and POWs. Once
the romushas were on board the Junyo Maru, it was
our turn. We sailed that afternoon. Not far from
Benkulu, Sumatra, we were torpedoed. Everybody
jumped into the water, but I couldn't swim. I waited
up on deck. A friend of mine went to the lifeboats,
which the Japanese were trying to launch. Instead
of being permitted to come along, they beat him on
the head with a hammer. He was probably dead by
the time he hit the water.

I was thinking: 'What am I going to do?'
Suddenly, I heard a very loud voice, where it came
from I had no idea, that said: 'Jump, Lex, you'll be
saved!' It scared me for a moment. It was the voice
of my father, who was out to protect me. He had
died when I was seven years old when his motorbike
crashed into a streetcar.

But the moment I heard that, I climbed down
to the water by way of the outdoor toilets. A chest
came floating by, about a square yard in size – as if
made to order! Several people joined me after a few
minutes. One was an American, who asked: 'Mind if
I join you?' 'Not at all.' Then he started counting

and when he came to 12, he said: 'That makes
me number 13. I don't think I care for that.
I'd better start looking for something else.'

Looking backwards, I noticed that the
uppermost part of the ship was black with
romushas, probably all people who couldn't
swim, just like me. But this lasted only a few
minutes. Then the ship broke into two and sank,
taking all those people with it. We tried to
keep ourselves and our little chest as far away
from the sinking ship as possible. The next day,
around 2:00 o'clock, we came alongside a Japanese frigate: Saved! We set course for Padang,
and along the way you could hear screaming and
hollering: 'Tolong! Help!' Sad to say, we were full
to capacity. I can still see it all before me.

Every time we'd be working on the railway,
we'd see those romushas all along the tracks asking
for help, their bellies distended from edema. They
had no medicine. That was awful. We were badly
off as well, but even so, we still had some medicine
while they had nothing at all. It certainly was a
pitiful sight. Whenever we had a break, I'd be in
the forest. But while foraging for vegetables there
you'd be frightened half to death from of all those
skulls of romushas just abandoned there. One fine
day, I came across a romusha lying underneath an
awning. He was already dead, his body half decomposed. I took pity on the man. I went up to the
Jap guard and said, 'Hey man, listen, there's a dead
romusha lying there, how about me burying him?'
He said to me: 'Oh, come off it, no need, forget it,
the tigers will eat him.' Well, I thought that was
just awful.

Peacetime never really did come to us
prisoners of war. Right after the Japanese surrender, we were hurriedly transported to the city of
Palembang. The Sumatran natives had started kill-
ing the Dutch in the city. The Japs were supposed
to keep law and order after a fashion. And we were
supposed to help out a bit. We were immediately
armed and got an Enfield, that long, stupid rifle,

---

1   See also the stories of Willem Punt
    and Willem Wildeman.

2   Port of Batavia, now Jakarta.

and khakis and shoes. Mind you, we paid for that stuff ourselves, about forty guilders or something. For all I know, he put it into his own pocket, that captain, I mean.

After that, me and eight guys had to go to Kramat prison camp in the city of Batavia to guard it against *peloppors*, those Indonesian freedom fighters. After all, I was a professional soldier, wasn't I? The first thing one of the guys did there was to go home. But he didn't see anybody. Then he asked his neighbor: 'Where's my family?' 'Oh, sir, they threw them down the well, all of them, and then they pelted them with stones.' So he went and looked, and yes, sure enough, stones. He got mad as hell. He then simply took his automatic rifle into a nearby native village and out of revenge shot everyone in sight.

I'd gotten married, meanwhile. In 1950 we left for the Netherlands. When we arrived in Rotterdam, it was between 10 and 15 degrees Celsius below zero. I think we disembarked around 10:00 in the morning, and we got an apple and a cup of pea soup. We went by bus, and our destination was the town of Simpelveld, in the South. It took hours and we got nothing else to eat. My wife was more than eight months pregnant. When we arrived at dusk at our government-arranged rental apartment in Simpelveld, the landlady pointed at my wife's belly and said: 'But that wasn't part of the bargain!' Just goes to show you how we were received!

Later on, I was transferred to a different apartment in the nearby town of Valkenburg. That was an inn that rented rooms. I was attending the air force academy in Nijmegen and I had to study at night. At 11:00 at night, however, they turned off the electricity. At 7:00 o'clock in the morning, I had to take my train. At that hour the inn hadn't opened yet and you were not supposed to go through there alone because the owner was afraid you'd lift something. This meant that you had to scale a two-meter high wall to get to the railway station. The only thing that place lacked was Japs. If it hadn't been for that I would have been a POW all over again.

In three years, we stayed in seven different apartments, which, except for one, were all terrible. The landlords pocketed enough rent money for keeping us, but they gave us nothing in return. Too crazy for words, especially when you think you've fought for queen and country, that you've been a POW, after which those guys make you go out and fight some more to make money for the national treasury! It's enough to make you cry! That's what drives you *loco*, man, it's enough to make you sick.

I told my kids: 'When you come right down to it, we're strangers here, you know. So you've got to keep the moral high ground, be better than these people here in Holland: Act better than them. Whenever there's a problem, make sure you have your facts straight. Make sure you know what's what and that you can earn your own living. That's why you've got to go to college. And I'll see to it that you can pay your tuition.' And that's just what they've all done, thank goodness. During all those years they went to college, I've not been on a holiday even once. I left the service when I turned 49, I retired. After that, I worked for the insurance bank to finance my kids' education.

I lost two uncles on the Junyo Maru, that's where I also lost my friend, but what grieves me more than that has been our reception afterwards, here in the Netherlands. You're Dutch, after all, even though you may have some Indonesian blood in your veins. You didn't expect them to treat you this way. In the bus, they asked us: 'Where did you learn to speak such excellent Dutch?' Those were the real insults, I think. It's the kind of thing that haunts you more than what you've experienced during the war. Don't you think I, too, have Dutch blood in my veins? Man, my great-grandfather was a baker in Rotterdam!"

Han de Bruïne

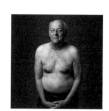

"A guy alone had about a snowball's chance in hell."

Born February 8, 1923, in Cimahi close to Bandung, Java. He grew up in the Dutch East Indies and in the Netherlands. In May 1944, he was among the first party to start work on the Sumatra Railway.
After the war he became an economist.

"Coming from Tanjung Priok on Java, I saw my first romushas when our ship arrived in Padang's Emmahaven,[1] Sumatra. They'd been on board our ship as well. If from nothing else, they died of heat exhaustion. There were those among them who committed suicide by jumping into the sea. The odd thing is that at the time it didn't make much of an impact on you, which is disgraceful. But being on board that ship made you fairly indifferent. You started walking around with blinders on. I had just that one goal: I've got to get out of here! And, I've got to have a cheese sandwich! Quite an obsession, don't you think?

In POW camp number 2, I was part of the burial detail. That wasn't such an appealing job. You had to keep the corpse's head upright while carrying it to the grave. If you didn't do that just right they'd empty out and you'd be covered in all that infected matter. As to the graves, there was a time the ground water stood so high that you had to keep them down with sticks because they started to float.

The thing that impressed me more than anything else during our imprisonment was the near total lack of 'gentlemen.' That was not something you'd expect, coming from a good school as I did, the fact that older people could be so uncivilized. I thought it a sad thing that many individuals had such a thin veneer of civilization. With a few notable exceptions, people in general proved disappointing. Here, man was reduced to a minimum. Don't get me wrong, I had a great deal of admiration for what the camp doctors were able to accomplish, for example. But although my own father was an officer, I've got to say that most officers in the POW camp didn't amount to much, though. You'd think you could expect a little support from them, but boy, they generally let us down.

Back in the Netherlands, I had my mind set on studying medicine. That had been my goal even in high school. But then, you see, in 1947 my wife and I got engaged and I did the math: That would mean first seven and then another four years of study, for I didn't want to go into general practice. So I went to study economics in Rotterdam instead. Later on, while working for Philips, I got my masters, which meant reading some 50 pages a day even if a business meeting lasted till 4:00 in the morning. After that was over and done with, we had oceans of time to ourselves.

I think the principal legacy of the war has been that I always wanted to move forward, to continue and never stop. That was already something I believed in back on the railway: I had to move on for I wanted to stay alive. Ever since, I've been planning not so much for the day after tomorrow as for the day after the next couple of years. I expected the same from my children. Perhaps it bothered them. Whenever things were not going well in school, I'd say something like: 'Why can't you do it, dummy?' Or: 'You're not planning to become dog catcher by any chance, are you?' Even to this day, although walking is becoming a bit more of a problem, when my wife and I are on vacation, the urge remains to keep going.

When our children went to college, I told them: 'I don't care if you become prime minister or what, as long as you make sure you become a member of a group or society you can depend on in the event anything happens.' That's probably

---

1 Now Telukbayur.

82

pretty close to the *kongsi*[2] strategy and philosophy. Some people truly exaggerate the idea of pulling together, but on the railway a guy alone had about a snowball's chance in hell. In that case, you had nobody to depend on and nobody to help you. Being part of a kongsi meant that one of you would always see to it that the food was equally divided and that everyone got a fair shake. Whenever you came across anything of value outside the camp, something useful, say, then you'd share that.

We didn't really begin talking about what happened until quite a bit later. For the longest time, we regarded it as a closed chapter. This was true even though my wife was facing the issue of her father having died at a young age on that torpedoed ship. Anyway, the more unpleasant aspects of the war didn't get talked about until a dozen or so years ago. Don't ask me why then exactly. As a couple, you sooner or later get to talk about this and that, after the children have left home. You go in search of your roots, as it were. We started going to reunions, where you heard more stories. You'd ask yourself, how was this again, and why do you think that happened? Pretty soon, I stopped going to the Sumatra meetings. Naturally, that was the place where you could tell one another: 'It was terrible, and more than anything, what they did to those romushas was outrageous.' But, really, it's not something you want to start wallowing in, I think.

I once signed on as a visiting lecturer. What people are taught here about history is shameful. I'm not sure, however, that I know how to tell those boys and girls exactly how things happened, because I'd run the risk of seeming pathetic. I ran into a psychologist who went on about shielding children from traumatic events and that sort of

thing. I was thinking: Oh, my God, here we have another devotee of Bastiaans.[3] Damned, that guy practically talked thousands of people into doing themselves in. Okay, maybe I'm a bit too cynical about all that. And I also think that my wife and I had the advantage that we both had been through it. And that both of my brothers survived it, as did my parents. And because we lived in The Hague right after the war, we were part of a community where things were commonly understood and didn't require endless discussion."

2   A small, tight unit of people who looked out for one another.

3   Professor Dr. J. Bastiaans, a controversial Dutch psychiatrist who became known for his treatment of war traumas using LSD, among other things.

Willem van Hasselt

"I've not gotten around to getting excited about it."

Born December 12, 1911, in Rotterdam. He left for the Indies in 1935 to work for the Colonial Bank. Then he became a forced laborer on the Burma Railway.
After the war, he was the director of a travel agency.
He died on January 29, 2003.

"Initially I was a prisoner of war in a camp situated on the Surabaya fair grounds. Next we ended up in Batavia, now called Jakarta, and then we were transported to Singapore, and after that the Burma thing started.

Everything in your life was turned topsy-turvy. You asked yourself if things could ever be set straight again. The fact that many of your friends shared the same fate didn't really help. If anyone were to ask me now, 'Did you emerge from that period as a totally changed person?' I'd find it difficult to give a concrete answer to that question. Everything sort of sneaked up on you, and as such it is impossible to tell what was really you and what was the result of external circumstances changing you. Did it leave deep traces in me? I've got to be honest, no, it didn't. At least not that I can remember. And in the event it did, life afterwards must have erased them. So many things have happened since then to shape me that I'm not sure anymore who I really am. I've had the great privilege of not only finding a dear wife but also of finding both my parents still alive when I returned from that whole situation to the Netherlands.

It was, of course, terribly unpleasant having to work for days on end laying those railroad tracks all the way through the jungle, up and down, it really was hard work most of the time. And I was really a bit of a weakling, I couldn't work all that much on account of me being on my back courtesy of dysentery. And those Japs were, of course, a bit of a pain. But there are plenty of annoying people in the Netherlands, too. Did the Japs really bother me all that much? They probably did, but I must have forgotten. My memory is very bad. Fact is I didn't have such a very hard time during those years. They never beat me to the ground or flogged me. At the most, they've struck me a couple of times, but no more than that. I can't remember ever having undergone anything evil at their hands. A few unpleasant things, sure, but I've always tried to imagine what we would have done if we had been the victors and we had had to deal with them, what would I have done in their place? Besides, it was the Koreans who bothered me more than anyone else. They were a nasty bunch of guys. The Japanese kept themselves more in the background, using those Koreans for gofers. But do I hate them? Well, that was their job, wasn't it? They were hired to beat those POWs with sticks. In addition, there was a sense of contempt, sort of, wondering whether they didn't have something better to do. It may sound silly, but I think we felt superior to those Koreans.

During those years I had the feeling: We'll just have to endure this for a while, but our time will come and then we'll settle our score with you. But when the war was over and done with, I had so many different things on my mind that I've not gotten around to getting excited about it. All of the Netherlands needed fixing up again. I arrived in Rotterdam on board the troopship Nieuw Amsterdam and saw the city where I'd been born – well, I can tell you, that devastation really took me aback. I was down and out financially, I really needed to get to work on my personal and professional life, and I truly didn't have any time to think about the war. And by now the whole subject is so remote that I find it difficult to talk about. Maybe I am a lucky man to have as few scars as I do.

Afterwards, I got to Japan on business once or twice. I absolutely do not recall anymore whether or not I was initially disinclined to go there. But we were all very astonished by the friendly and hearty reception we got there. I even did try to talk about the war with those people there. When I got to Japan the first time, I was very interested to hear how they had experienced the war. And the answer I got was nothing short of a total vacuum! The fact was that they had not truly experienced that war at all. I had to explain to them that I'd been working on their Burma Railway, and they found that rather interesting. Then again, it would be wrong to say that they were very impressed by my story, not at all, ha, ha, really not. It wasn't as if I had inspired them to tell me their side of the story. I really don't recall whether or not I was annoyed or angered by this, but I don't think I was."

Leo Kollmann

"I really have not suffered any
aftereffects at all."

Born October 17, 1923, in Semarang, Java.
Worked on the Burma Railway during the war.
After World War II, he became a professional
soldier and took part in the so-called police
actions, the Dutch military actions aimed at
fighting Indonesian independence.

"They took us POWs to the IVth and IXth battalion[1]
in Cimahi. A couple of Ambonese soldiers got shot
there. But I wasn't there when it happened. I've
never wanted to witness anything of the sort again.
We earlier on had an execution of a certain Peetoom
and Braam who had run away and had been cap-
tured by the Japanese. They were put up against the
barbed wire and shot.

On October 17, 1942, right on my birthday,
they shipped us to Singapore. A couple of months
later we were shipped to Rangoon. Those transports
were hell. Once in Burma, in camp 108,[2] we worked
on that famous railway bridge across the River
Kwai, a wooden bridge planted straight on the rocks
below and only held together with cramp irons.
Sure, it was in our own interest that we did the job
right for we had to cross that same bridge by train
ourselves. That's where we had our first air raids.
Of course, the Americans and the English were out
to bomb that bridge and not our camp. One day I
was ordered to replace one of the damaged bridge
supports. So there I was with a friend of mine, sitting way up on that pillar. And what do you know,
right there and then one of these rotten little allied
spotter planes passed over. This could only mean
one thing – that another bombardment was on its
way. Well, what could we do? We were fortunate
that it was high tide, so we were able to leap into
the water. That was quite a jump, you know, well
over five yards. And you had to make sure that you
landed properly. After that I've never been in a
swimming pool again, not in all that deep water.

And then there were those moron guards!
Many of them were Koreans. One of them was
called 'Rubber Lips,' for they all had nicknames,
you know. He was one of the guards assigned to
the transport ahead of ours, the one that got
torpedoed. And those prisoners naturally tried to
push every Jap's head under water till he drowned.
So this guy was out for revenge and he'd beat somebody to the ground at the slightest provocation.

The Japanese technicians, they were quite
reasonable. There was this Japanese orderly, for
instance, called Yasasan, who was a Catholic.
Whenever we celebrated mass with the chaplain on
a Sunday, he would come to communion. He also
had guard duty, and his post was near the hospital
barracks. He used to buy things for the sick there,
such as eggs, and sugar. I'll never forget that man.

Quite a number of my friends passed away.
That does something to you, you know, your buddy
passing away, it gets to you. But after a while, you
still have not quite forgotten him, but it's history.
Done. Time goes on, and you've got to think of
yourself. Everybody lived for himself. You've got
to make sure that you come out of it alive. There
must have been several hundred men in that camp,
and on any given day at least 15 men would die
of tropical infections and especially malaria. Well
then, there came a time when that left you cold.
Someone would sound the Last Post, but that, too,
would leave you indifferent.

In that same camp I watched an Australian
surgeon operate. Tropical sores. If they had pen-
etrated too far, an amputation was called for. Don't
ask me what they used for instruments, nothing but
dull saws. They did it out in the open, surrounded
by green mosquito netting. But that man did a
wonderful job of it, nothing like, let's cut him up.

1   This is what the barracks were called.

2   The number refers to the distance in kilometers
     from the start of the railway.

He'd explain the entire make-up of such a leg. He gave us a lecture in anatomy. My wife finds it odd that I still love watching medical programs like that on TV.

If I may be honest with you, and I'm not boasting about it in the least, I really have not suffered any aftereffects at all. I applied for financial assistance from an agency that helps war victims. Two female doctors appeared and they tried to get me so far as to admit that I was traumatized. Well, come off it, the moment I was liberated my only aim was to make a future for myself. The last thing I wanted was to start complaining about my aches and pains. And sure enough, I succeeded in that. But I couldn't convince the dear ladies of that. Well, either you can fake it, or you can't. And I just can't. You hear about people coming away from a war with a great deal of stress, such as with the UN military coming back from Lebanon. But wait a minute, dear people, you know what you're letting yourself in for. Didn't you sign up for the army? Those are the consequences if you are a professional. I may well be an oddball, but I find it hard to imagine that is something that will traumatize you. I find it all a bit far-fetched and a bit of a publicity stunt. It's not something I need.

Oh, sure, I did get some financial assistance from that agency in the end, for they told me: 'Mr. Kollman, sir, you're a war victim.' And that is true, of course! Have I not been a POW? I ended up joining the organization for Dutch military war victims. So that makes me a war victim, too. The only thing is, it didn't leave me with any traumas.

There are moments, of course, when something resurfaces. That's inevitable. Take the annual memorial service on August 15 in The Hague, for example. I like going there, even though I know it will come to tears. They sing Ave Maria, and someone says The Lord's Prayer in Malay, that's so beautiful, you know. And when they sing the National Anthem – well wait a minute... Excuse me... There. I'm alright again. Yes, that's where

I commemorate my friends. And my oldest brother, who died during the war. We don't know where or how that happened. He was a medic with the Red Cross. I suspect he was butchered and tortured by the Japanese. Yes, on a day like that the thought enters your mind and you say to yourself, darn it, I've lived through quite a mess, haven't I? What a lucky man I have been.

I've never discussed it with my sons. They never asked. There's no need for them to know the misery I've been through. That's all in the past. And it doesn't bother me in the least. Thank goodness."

Ben de Lizer

**"What you really want to forget,
you remember best."**

Born October 27, 1920, in Semarang, Java.
He was a professional soldier before and
after World War II. Shipped out to Pekanbaru,
Sumatra, in May 1944. He died on
September 30, 2004.

"On March 6, 1942, we were holding the Ciater
position,[1] waiting for the Japanese to attack.
Around 5:30 we had to assemble to get bread.
All of a sudden the Japanese started shooting at
us. There were no officers to be seen anywhere.
Not even NCOs. They all got away, to a man. And
the boys, the soldiers, they all stayed. Some
surrendered, such as a certain Assendelft, with
a white hanky tied to his rifle. That's when the
Japs advanced. But some of us fought on and
managed to open fire on them still. But don't
you think there should have been a commander
present? What about leadership? Instead, everybody fought on his own.

The Japs made a swift assault and took all
of us prisoner, some 40 or 50 men. They took us
into the forest. When we arrived, we had to take
off our leggings, and they tied us up in bunches of
three. Me too, with a certain Kolk and Frederiks.
Then the Japs mounted two machine guns and
started shooting. Some of the guys started praying
out loud, some called for their mother, and some
for their wives. Because they felt they're going to
be killed. At the time, I didn't have any thoughts
whatsoever. None, no thoughts at all. Was I scared?
No, I wasn't scared, either. All I knew was: I'll
survive this. That's the thought I had when they
started shooting. I got three bullets in my back and
left shoulder and I fell forward, with the two others on top of me. Then the Japs made sure we were
dead. Those who gave any sign of life were either
bayoneted, got hit with a rifle butt, or got a bullet.

It was war, after all. If we had taken as many
Japanese prisoners, we probably would have shot
them, too. Too many prisoners of war. They had
to get rid of us.

After a couple of hours I tried to get away
from that spot because the smell of human blood
is terrible. I went to try and get help, but I wan-
dered about lost for six days instead. My wounds
began to stink already. Three days without food
or drink. Meanwhile, my mother had already been
notified of my death. On the sixth day I arrived
in Dago, where they took me to the hospital.

In May of 1944, when I went to Pekanbaru,
my wounds were only partially healed. They still
contained fine bone splinters. But I was still a
young man! We had to carry railway ties and make
bridge supports. Or we had to make poles. We had
groups of five guys who went into the forest to
cut trees. I belonged to a group that had to drag
the felled trees to the road. There we loaded them
onto trucks. Five tree trunks a day. They were cut
up into railroad ties. I was in camp number 1 all
that time. I carried the tree trunks. I also had to
carry rails, together with 11 or 12 men, just that
one rail. On your shoulder, yes, on the good one,
not the left shoulder. Wasn't that bad, really, it
had already started to heal.

Following the Japanese surrender, we all
got a medical check-up. Well, as long as you could
walk, breathe or eat, you passed the test, even if
you were sick. They just made sure you could take
up arms again.[2] How else would they have been
able to assemble an army this fast? Well, naturally,
by using the former POW!

I was serving with an intelligence unit when
I heard there was this guy somewhere in a village
just three miles from where I was. So I went there.
I interrogated him. For a week. He was a so-called

---

1   See also the story of Dolf Winkler.

2   During the so-called police actions against
    the Indonesian freedom fighters.

instructor for the Indonesian army, who had troops there. Then I got a phone call telling me he'd be taken to HQ in Palembang for further interrogation. A week later HQ sent him back with the message that I was to shoot him: 'let him go take a leak.'

I said: 'Couldn't you do that yourself, on the way here?' After all, that was a possibility, don't you think? But they came anyway. So there I was, stuck with this guy. I couldn't very well let him go. A lousy situation, you know. I fed him all that first week. Took care of him, talked to him, stuff like that. And now I had to go out and shoot him. Terribly difficult. He walked ahead of me in open field. I readied my rifle, but what do you know, he saw its shadow. So I pulled back. I gave him a smoke. And he smoked. He happened to be near a tree, in the shade. It just took that one shot. In my report I wrote: 'While trying to escape.'

It's not an easy thing to kill someone, you know. But if you've done it once, then it doesn't scare you anymore. If anyone were to hurt me now, I'd gun him down without compunction. I don't care, you know. I'd do it just like that. Back then, I couldn't. Back then, I would have said to myself, gosh, darn it, that's a fellow human being. But I'm not sorry. Well, sorry, yes, I was sorry in the beginning. But now that's behind me, everything. How else am I going to live with it? I can't very well be walking around with a bunch of guilt. I'm not that feeble-minded, you know. I try to maintain a positive view of life. Most people don't know that I just have the one lung left. But I still get a lot done on that one lung, you know.

During the night, that's when the dreams and things like that start. What about? I don't quite know. But invariably I begin to scream. It bothers my wife and it bothers our friends, too, when they're staying with us. Once I made such a racket that I woke myself up. I am afraid our neighbors might hear me. This sort of thing is still happening! As recently as last week. But I never remember what I dream about.

I never ever think about that war. I want to forget the whole thing, you know, but then again, what you really want to forget, you remember best. But in the event the whole thing were to start all over again, if my country were to need me again, then I'd join up again, no doubt. You never forget how to handle a gun. I'm not sure what makes people act this way. It's all because of the war. It's because I've already killed people, I think. But death doesn't scare me anymore. If you've got to die, then you've got to die."

Chris Moonen

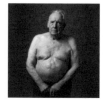

"All of my senses were fully alert.
I never panicked."

Born January 31, 1917, in Dordrecht, the Netherlands. Originally a carpenter by trade, the Great
Depression forced him to sign up with the KNIL,
the colonial army of the East Indies. He was
shipped out to become a forced laborer on the
Burma Railway in October 1942. After the war,
he became a ship's carpenter, a concierge and
a chauffeur.

"We underestimated the Japanese. That was the result of our own ignorant propaganda: The Japanese were nothing but little men wearing spectacles, with poor eyesight, who certainly couldn't shoot straight. Their planes were made of wood.

Well, we sure got a nasty surprise when we saw the planes they really possessed. Later on, we also got the notion that the Japanese were ferocious, Rambo-style fighters and such. Of course they weren't anything of the kind. Those Japanese would only accomplish something whenever there were great hordes of them. A small Japanese patrol, however, as I experienced later on, wasn't nearly as courageous. Small groups of them were probably also afraid of the jungle. Just like the Dutch.

I went to Rangoon on the Tacoma Maru.[1] A filthy, rotten boat it was, crammed with people, lots of yelling by the Japs, and hitting people left and right. Some of the guys took their protests to the Japs, something I stopped doing right away. It was the stupidest thing you could do. All you got for your trouble was a sound beating. The worst thing was that they'd use heavy sticks or rifles to beat you with, and that really inflicted a lot of damage on a man's body. The thing I learned while in Jap custody was to stay on the lookout and to count the days. And trying to figure out what his weak spot was. That was something you had to exploit right away. If, for example, there were women in the vicinity you had to point that out to the Japs: 'Naniedeska?,' what's that? The slightest diversion was enough to make them look the other way. One of their weak spots was that they admired someone who could lift something heavy, for example, or who was very strong. And indeed, I was someone like that back then.

In Burma, we went to Thanbyuzayat for that railway project. You should know that we got up at early daybreak. Our breakfast consisted of a thin gruel. It was water with rice. Lots of water. Then we'd have roll call. That was always terrible, the head-count would go on forever, with many repeats, for the Japs couldn't count. When that was finally over and done with, then we'd be up and away, off to work in gangs, and that often meant walking for miles. Not at first, when the work site was nearby, but the job was increasingly further away from the camp, till we had reached our limit. And then, all of a sudden, we'd have to move camp. All day long you'd have been working, and then we'd have to get ready that same evening to go on to yet another camp, from camp 70 to camp 108, which meant walking for 24 miles, barefoot through the jungle.

The work itself was physically hard and for a lot of people mentally difficult as well, especially for those who despite everything would be asking themselves all kinds of questions. I've overheard conversations like: 'Well, Jan, we're not going to make it; we're only getting this many calories per day, and the human body requires that many calories to survive. It's easy enough to figure out when you're going to die.' That was something that never worried me. The thing that was important and did preoccupy me was getting a bit extra to eat. In the jungle, you could scrounge and forage for vegetables, or mushrooms, or snakes, all kinds of things. Large larvae, which you'd find in rotten wood. You'd skewer them on a stick and, bingo, grill them over

1   See also the story of Henk Wiersma.

a fire. That we copied from the guys with an Indies background. I quickly adapted myself to living in the bush. There were not that many Dutchmen who felt comfortable in the *utan*.[2] Sixty feet into the jungle, and they'd be lost already. Not me, though. I could just walk in and then as easily walk out again. I was a hunter. 'Nature lover' would be stretching it, but a hunter, too, is a nature lover of sorts.

After the war I stayed on in the army. I took part in all of the police actions.[3] That was definitely my own choice. Even when another platoon went on patrol. 'Oh, are you going tomorrow? Mind if I come along?' Of course, we did have our share of dead and wounded. But I sailed through it in one piece.

Some people ask me: 'Moonen, were you never afraid?' Oh yes, I've been afraid alright. Walking out there at night, I'd invariably have this tight feeling in my stomach, and that was fear. But the moment the firing started that just disappeared, and all that remained was a kind of anger. And I'd be very alert then. I never panicked. All of my senses were fully alert. And whether I was hunting or on patrol, when things got tense, I knew how to shoot fast and straight.

For me personally, the period right after the war was a good time. My entire platoon was made up of Indonesians. I've been to several reunions and when they asked what I missed more than anything, I told them: 'I miss my Indonesian buddies, the ones I got to know there.'

Speaking of a reunion like that, each time it proved to be a bit of a disappointment. Well, what is a reunion, after all, other than seeing your old acquaintances again? That wasn't the case with me. All of my acquaintances are either in Indonesia or they are dead. What about those from my Burma Railway days? Well, you'd be correct in saying that we had thousands of people there. But I believe that every former prisoner of war shares my feeling that you were not truly aware of that many people. You were there in that camp, and life actually took place within a terribly small circle of people. People hardly ever talked, for there was nothing to talk about, and everybody was preoccupied with his own thoughts. The largest *kongsi*[4] I ever belonged to consisted of just three men, one who cooked, one who bartered and traded, and one who saw to it that we had something to eat. The more people in a group, the greater the discontent. Most of these outsiders were just occasional friends. Most of them I never saw again. It's not easy to put one's finger on it, but I really think those friendships there were different from those in the Netherlands. If one guy over there got into trouble then you'd try to get him back on his feet as soon as possible. Still, you couldn't very well help him with everything, for you yourself were in fact just a, well, how shall I put it... Let me put it this way, in a kongsi one might get sick and be hospitalized, or one might die – and none of this was very exceptional because people died every day. We even had a routine: When you returned from work at night, you'd ask: 'How many?' 'Eight.' How come people talked so little? Well, there wasn't really anything new to be said. What was new was that eight people had died that day.

This had its consequences. The dead had to be buried, and that had to happen that very same day, and so there had to be people to do that. And who were they? Those were the people still fit enough to do the job. That included me. It was something one did automatically. It wasn't so bad to bury someone because he was dead, after all. He only thing I disliked was having a cholera epidemic. All those patients had to be cremated. Then some 50 men would go there, lickety-split. Some of them would gather dry bamboo from the forest, because we needed a huge fire, and then you'd have

2   The Jungle.

3   Dutch military actions against Indonesian soldiers
    fighting for their independence.

4   A small, tight unit of people who looked out for
    one another.

to lift the dead and toss them into the fire. Well, it wasn't something I enjoyed. Still, it could not be avoided, that had to happen. And you had to be resigned to the things that had to happen. I think that some of the guys who had to do such a thing might have gotten nightmares later on. Not me, you understand. Sure, it had its effect on me, too, but never for very long, a couple of days, maybe. I'm not that much of an emotional man. Whoever is dead is dead, that's what I think.

I rarely get excited about things anymore. Things such as racial segregation and other non-sense, such as politics, none of it interests me in the slightest, it's all a little nonsensical. What's important is that people should be able to live together without criticizing each other. Not: He's a Muslim, and he's a Jew, and he's a Catholic and he's a Protestant, come off it. Some people really do get carried away, don't you think?

I do believe that the war made me more tolerant about some things. Then again, the reverse is quite true also. I worked for this shipbuilding company, and we had a fellow there who was dishonest, he stole from people. I noticed that, and I went for him straight away. I gave him one hell of a beating. What you think, actually, is that if you had been a POW and he had been caught stealing, then you would have attacked him, too.

After I turned 65, I got into the scrap business. What else should I have done? Sit in a nook with a book? Don't get me wrong, I like reading, but not for a whole day. I like to keep busy. So I met this guy in the scrap iron business. He looked at me in a funny sort of way and said: 'What on earth could you be wanting?' I told him: 'Don't you guys have something that needs taking apart?' 'Yeah, those big generators, for one.' 'Well then, just explain to me how to go about that.' And he told me: 'You first have to batter and break those jackets with a sledgehammer, that's all cast iron. Then you've got to remove the armature, the copper.'

And that's what I've been doing till I turned 80. Then my knees began to bother me, so that's when I went to the doctor's eventually. He told me: 'Degenerative arthritis.' I said: 'Degenerative arthritis, what's that?' 'Worn out.' I said: 'What can we do about it?' 'There's nothing we can do about it.' So there you are. Well, in the old days that sort of thing happened to working people all the time, didn't it? I very rarely talk about the war at all.

Talking with Henk Wiersma goes something like this: 'Say, Henk, how did they do things in the artillery?' – that was his outfit, mine was the infantry. 'Well, we did things in such and such a fashion, and I was stationed there and there.'

We do indeed talk about the war, but only in a summary fashion. And that is, let me explain, because those camps were all equally miserable. I couldn't very well say: 'That's where we were hungry, and there we were hungry too, but over in that place we were hungriest of all.'

As for my wife, sure, we often talk. But those conversations only concern the time before the war, when she was little. And then there's a hiatus of sorts, something neither of us talks about, and that is the war period. Crazy. And why? In the first place, her war experience is one of true poverty, very little to eat, and sickness. She had little brothers, who are all of them dead, a little sister, also dead. No, that's an unpleasant story, I don't want to tell you about it. Don't ask me why not. Listen, of course I talk about Burma, about everything living there. Take grasshoppers, for instance: Just fry them a bit and they make a fine meal."

Ko Muller

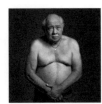

**"I only keep wondering:
For how much longer?"**

Born May 16, 1918, in Semarang, Java. He was a professional army man who got sent to the Burma Railway. After that, he was in Singapore until the war's end. He was in the military during the the police actions, fighting Indonesian independence. After being admitted to a military hospital, he received medical leave for psychological reasons, spent the next year and a half in a clinic and was dismissed from the army. He then worked as a cook and in a copy center. In the 1970s, he had another psychological breakdown and was treated by the psychiatrist Professor Bastiaans. He died on June 25, 2005.

"My friend Ferry and I managed to sneak out of the prison camp. We did that a couple of times, and always with a full moon, because you couldn't see a thing otherwise. From those of us who had something to trade we took a shirt, a pair of pants, sometimes even a wedding ring to sell. What they wanted in exchange was salt, sugar, and tobacco. And our camp doctor asked us: 'Try and get some MMB tablets, they're multi-purpose. I could really help a lot of people with those.' That's what we did. And then we climbed back into camp. That was in the middle of the night, around 1:00 or 2:00. It always went well, sure enough, until it went differently.

    We were on our way back. Again, a full moon. I said to Ferry: 'You go ahead first.' Whenever we came back inside, we'd have to calm down because your heart would beat in your throat, and only after that would we take turns going on. By the time I thought, I'm sure he's safely through by now – because you had to pass through the Japanese section – I would go. By the light of the full moon I suddenly saw a shiny reflection of something up above me. That could only mean one thing: A Jap rifle with a bayonet on it. And the Jap had spotted me. That was a very, very difficult moment right there. Because you knew that you'd be shot if you were caught. At that moment, all in a one flash, I saw my entire life go by, from childhood on, parents, brothers, sisters, everything. Yes, sure, a farewell of sorts. There is, however, a difference between one Jap and another, and that difference is that there are good ones and lowlifes. This must have been a good one. Normally, if anything out of the ordinary happens as it did in this case, such a Jap guard gets nervous and starts to holler and so wakes up the entire barracks. Not this one, however, for he whispered: 'Psst, what have you got there?' This Jap language was little more than a hodgepodge, you know, a mixture of Japanese, English, Malay and a few words of Dutch, so it was a challenge to understand. 'Where did you come from?' I told him: 'From the outside.' 'From the outside?!' Invariably, this would be followed by one of their Japanese expletives, in this case *'Bageiro,'* you must be crazy. 'What have you got there?' 'Food.' 'Food?' And again: 'Bageiro. Why?' 'Because we've got to work very hard for you and we're not getting enough to eat.' Ferry, whom I didn't see until I stood near the Jap, was opening his bag, and then I said to the Jap: 'You want some, too?' Then again: 'Bageiro,' and in English, 'no good, no good.' And then, all of a sudden, still in English: 'OK, go!'

    Well, sir, if you hear that while expecting a bullet, when you hear him say 'go,' then it's as if you're going through the floor. 'OK, go, go!' Well then, we closed our small bags and slowly walked away. And then we'd stop and turn around. 'OK, go!' Even now, many years later, at night, around 2:00 o'clock, I'm awake. Every night. When I go to bed, I fall asleep. Around 2:00, I wake up. And then I don't sleep anymore. I may doze off a little, at the most. And I count the hours: 2:00, 2:30, 3:00, 3:30, and so on. The same every night, ever since that time. Yes, well. 'Go.'

You should see my bedroom, it's like a fortress. On my night stand I've got a Rambo dagger, from the Marines. And next to my bed a short samurai sword, sharp as a razor. And I'll never lie in bed with my face to the wall, but always facing the door. They're not going to get me!

Then we got word of the Japanese surrender. No celebrations where we were, just apathy. Nobody was shouting and dancing the way they did in the Netherlands, as they often show on TV, with people happily taking to the streets. Right away, Sukarno declared the independence of the Republic of Indonesia, and people started getting butchered: Old folks, women, and children. Well, then we realized that something had to be done! Army battalions were thrown together overnight. We got a physical check-up. Well, hardly, they didn't even so much as touch us. All they said was: Passed, passed, passed. How on earth could a doctor pass all those guys after they'd spent three and a half years in total misery? Here they were, with three and a half years' worth of pent-up hatred, pent-up degradation, slavery, you name it. And so you got put in a uniform, they stuffed a rifle into your hands, and you found yourself once again facing an enemy whom you knew had butchered your old folks, women and children. Then what do you get? You're no longer a human being, you're just an animal. Then you kill every single one of them, everyone you run into.

During a fight on the small island of Mendanau between Banka and Belitung, we suddenly heard something rustle. We didn't bother to look, we just kept firing. They were mere boys, aged between twelve and sixteen. Child soldiers. Ouch.

My psychiatrist, Professor Bastiaans, told us: 'You all worked yourselves to death after the war in order to suppress precisely that sort of thing. You did not want to think about it. But there comes a time when you are done working, and then you're finished. And that's when you have a breakdown. Bang. And that's when all of that comes to the surface.' That's true, too. Whenever I came home from work at night, I was totally burned out. Not worth a dime. I'd spent all of my energy back on the job. And for over 35 years, every single day, I walked around with a bursting headache. Despite that, I've never stayed home once.

My son frequently tells me: 'Why don't you just ignore all that stuff?' But TV, the paper, radio, everything conspires to remind you of those times. How on earth can anyone hope to ignore it? I'll be honest with you, when 9-11 happened, Bin Laden's attack on America, I had a difficult time of it, very difficult. I was thinking: darn it, here we've finally got the misery of the war put behind us, and now it's starting all over again. Wrong, very wrong.

Before I went to Bastiaans, there would be this wall in front of me. I kept going till I banged my head into that wall. I never got any further, let alone climb over it. In that clinic they got me to the point where I could get over it and see the other side of that wall. But if you were to ask what has changed since that treatment? Nothing, in fact. For if I still wake up every night at 2:00 o'clock, if I still have to lie in bed facing the door, and if I still have a dagger and a sword by my bedside, then nothing has really changed, has it? I just keep wondering: For how much longer?"

Ko Muller wrote about his experiences during and after the war in a book called *Doorbraak naar het onvoltooid verleden* ("Breakthrough to an Unfinished Past"), self-published, ISBN 90-802347-1-0

Ferrie Portier

"I was fighting for my life! That's all!"

Born May 15, 1916, in Malang, Java. Employed before the war by the HVA trading company in Amsterdam, the largest of its kind in the Indies. As a POW, he was sent to work on the Burma Railway in May 1942.

After the war, he was among other things once again employed by the HVA, then chief of the motorized transportation service in Surabaya and Banjuwangi, director of a shipyard in New Guinea, and, in the Netherlands, a customs officer.

"Following our surrender, they shipped me to Burma in the very first group. We first worked on the airfield at Tavoy. And after that we had to walk to the north, to Thanbyuzayat. That's where the Burma Railway began.

We were working in Wagale. That's where I bolted. Whatever gave me the idea to run off? Well, already back in Tavoy I'd been thinking: Hey, Tavoy, that's close to Colombo, Ceylon – close to, that is, several thousand kilometers by sea – and maybe I can steal a sail boat. But the west monsoon was blowing, so that was bad. So I ended up working on the railroad. Once there, you were nothing but an animal. They kicked you, gave you no food, nothing. You were nothing, you had nothing. And I just couldn't stand it there, with those Japanese.

That's when I got my chance. The Japs had cows, for slaughter. They were looking for a cowboy. Now it so happened that my grandfather had been a butcher, so ever since I was small I've seen how they do that. I was thinking: hey, that's something for me, then I'll be done with that railway and I can look at our surroundings.

One evening in September 1942, our commander arrived. He'd been enjoying a few days of beatings with the Japs to make him sign a document promising that we'd do nothing against the Japs and wouldn't run away. And he had to see to it that we'd also sign. However, if you signed and still ran away, then you were a goner for sure.

That's when I decided that I would skedaddle that same evening, for on the next day we had to sign. I'm saying "I", but there were the four of us. I first sounded out Piet van Heemert, a real Indies guy, a fine man and a military police officer: 'Van Heemert, you know how to sail a boat.' In addition, Hoffman, who could find his way in the jungle. Then myself, I knew a little about the area. And Schuurman.

Well, you know, there was nothing to escaping from prison camp, because the Japs didn't have any guards. Where could you go? Nothing but jungle. Malaria. Two months earlier, seven Australians had escaped. They were brought back that afternoon by the Burmese, who got 50 *rupees* a head. The Aussies first were beaten horribly. Then they were bayoneted. Right in front of us.

Still, we wanted to risk it. All we had in the way of food was rice. And an ax, and a machete. We walked quite a ways through the riverbed so as not to leave any tracks. And after that, God help us, we went into the bush. And the bush is nothing but one dark cavern. Only at noon did we see a glimmer of sunshine. We had no way of determining our direction. And we were terribly afraid. By God, you really didn't know what to do. The first two weeks were absolute misery. It was the rainy season and you couldn't make a fire, because smoke is something you smell from a great distance. So we kept on walking, hoping for the best. We checked to see which way the rivers ran and such. Because water runs down to the coast, that gave some sense of direction. And after 15 days, we were back at Wagale. We had made a complete circle!

Then we walked more in a southern direction. At a certain moment, we must have been on the outside for over a month by then, we spotted a hut. There is always rice there. But we could not afford to meet any people. Because you never knew if they would give you away. After all, they got money to turn us in.

Look, Burma, they say, is where the Burmese live. But there are over 14 tribes there, all of them dependent of one another, same as in the Dutch Indies. So this area was inhabited by the *Karen*. They are a mountain people, fairly stocky and sturdy. I look like a Karen, so it was my turn. I went there and the man didn't speak one word of English, all he said was 'Village, English.' And I said to him: 'Eat,' and 'We are not Japanese. We are Malays, coolies.' For there were romushas there, too. He gave us some rice. Then we went with him to this 'village.'

The people there were actually the best guys I've ever met anywhere. We came to the hut of Karen who spoke some English. The headman said: 'The Japanese have promised money if we point you out. But we are not going to. But tomorrow we take you to our center.' That was called Kyaing, about 50 miles away, in the Amherst district. But when we got there, they told us: 'You can not stay here, because nearby are Japanese. We will take you somewhat further away, to a camp of runaway military men.' There were all sorts of types and all kinds of riffraff there. In fact, it was a pack of robbers.

Then what? Van Heemert said: 'We'll go to that village of robbers and we'll train them to fight for when the English get here, or the Chinese.' So that's where we stayed. And we attacked Japanese police stations, five at least, and we turned out to be a pretty good unit.

How did we get through it all? You know that you're wanted, you know that there are others hunting you down, you spend your days and nights worrying about the slightest noise. My instincts and my hearing are such that I can hear it if anybody is walking through the forest kilometers away. After we attacked a police post, we would all split up and go into the jungle. Once I spent three months on a little *tampat* [1] up in the mountains. Completely alone. When I had nothing to eat, well, then I didn't eat. I've eaten young grass. And even there it was dangerous, for there were lots of wild animals such as tigers, bears, and particularly snakes. And if you had fallen ill or if you'd accidentally eaten something poisonous, then you're dead. That almost did me in. I constantly had to be on the lookout to stay alive.

Hoffman left us quite early on. He was a great guy. But a bit too good. He said: 'If I go it alone, I'll be safer.' And left just the three of us. They murdered him later on, killed in action, just like that. But somebody else joined us in his place: Knoestler. He had escaped, too, together with three officers. Those three were apprehended and shot. But not Knoestler. I don't know how he did it, but I didn't trust him a bit.

One of the robber chiefs liked me particularly. He told me: 'They can't touch me, for I've got amulets here.' Karen are tattooed all over their body, except for their anus. 'See to it that you get tattooed also. It's a sure way to stay alive.' But I didn't like the idea. So he gave me a shirt covered with all kinds of signs and symbols.

That silly shirt saved my life. On the last day that I was a free man, in September or October of 1944, the Japs and their men were after us with dogs and machetes, and the circle kept getting smaller and smaller. Then I said to Van Heemert: "Piet, you and I are going to make it. But not if those two stay with us!" One of them, Schuurman, was night blind, because of malnutrition. And Knoestler was altogether too stupid to... well, let's just say that if you took him a 100 yards in a different direction, he'd be unable to find his way home. He kept running this way and that like a stuck *tjeleng* [2], not knowing where to go. They were useless. We could have headed south. "Piet, shall

---

1   A sleeping mat.

2   A wild pig.

I shoot them?" I had the one rifle with four bullets in it. Then Van Heemert said: "No, in for a penny, in for a pound." Okay. So I threw away the rifle. Schuurman was a good guy. He was a special person to me, also after the war. I never told him I'd been on the verge of shooting him. I did take a closer look at his daughter later on, though. It would have been terrible having to tell her I knocked off her dad. I still meet his wife regularly. But I managed to forgive myself later on. Had I done it, it would have been in a state of momentary madness, seeing that circle get smaller all the time, and then seeing those two helpless people. It would have been an easy death for them.

But speaking of that silly shirt, there I noticed those guys getting closer and closer. They had dogs, sabers, all kinds of machetes, and so on. And all of a sudden there's this Burmese guy running into me. He had a rifle. He was very nervous, for I had the reputation of being a holy man of sorts. I'd been out there all this time, and they simply couldn't believe it. They simply couldn't believe that you'd been on the run for over two years. Anyway, the guy fired: A dud! Again. Misfired again! The guy gave out a loud yell, threw the thing away, and ran off as if he'd seen a ghost, no less. Then I went to look at the rifle. It turned out to be mine, with those four bullets, two of which proved to be duds!

Well, then the Japs arrived, and that's when I got the beating of my life. And then they handed us over to their commander of the *Kempetei*.[3] That's where the truth came out. 'Maybe you are spies sent in from British India. But certainly you are not the guys who escaped from Wagale. It's simply impossible that you've been on the outside for over two and a half years.' We said: 'We never lifted a finger against you, no, we would not have dared!' But they still did not believe us. Then they interrogated the Karen chief, Maung Mela his name was, and he said: 'These people are harmless, they've been working for us.'

They really tortured him, butchered him so to speak. But Maung Mela never changed his story. The next day, they poured kerosene over him and set him on fire. And even the Japs paid him their last respect. As they were burning him, they saluted him. How on earth is that possible? And we were thinking, well, we would have screamed well before being treated like this. But not Maung Mela. He didn't make a sound. He left a wife and a son. Those Karen are a great people. I told my daughter, whose name is Karen for that very reason: "If ever those people get their freedom, we'll go there." I've praised the Karen to the sky and it has rubbed off for she's an anthropologist.

Some vignettes of our stay with the Kempetai: They'd put you into a crate. It was impossible to either stand or sit in it. It was one yard high, one yard wide. Once a day, they let you out for a pee. Well, that's when I caught malaria. I sat there shaking like a leaf. A low-level Kempetai officer, who could hit like the best, asked me: 'Are you sick?' He returned with two blankets and some quinine. Then you ask yourself, is he crazy? Here's a guy who at one point beats the hell out of you, who cheerfully hits you over your bare skull, and then comes to your aid like this!

I was being interrogated by a different guy. Sits there, laughing. Gives me a smoke. And just as I'm ready to light up, he hits me so hard that I flip around. So there you were. Sometimes he'd laugh, and sometimes he'd yell. Your headache was so severe you couldn't open your eyes. I may seem even-keeled, but I was seething with fear. Take this, for example: When we were interrogated by the Kempetai, they made me dig a hole there 30 times. They told me: 'Now you're going to die.' But then it doesn't happen. And they stood there and laughed.

I tried to commit suicide. When they caught me. We were lying on the floor, and I said: 'They're going to kill us tomorrow anyway, you know what, we are going to commit suicide.' I still had a bit of a razor blade hidden in my *sarong*. 'Well, Piet, what

3   The Japanese Gestapo.

do you think? You are the oldest. Do you want them to do you in, or do you want to kill yourself?' 'Do it myself.' 'Schuurman, what do you think?' 'Yes, me too.' Only Knoestler didn't want to. So I said to him: 'That's your business. They'll probably set fire to you.' To Van Heemert I said: 'You know, it's easy enough, Piet. All you do is cut and it's over. You cut yourself and stay calm. You'll just fall asleep.' That's pure fantasy. Secretly, I was scared to death. Then Piet said: 'Do you want to help me do it?' He lacked the courage, see. Now I can easily enough shoot a man, but that I didn't want to do. At some stage he said: 'No. Maybe we'll get saved. We're not going to do it.' But I don't know even half how hard I had been pleading to be released from it all, pleading just to die.

After about two months, they took us to headquarters in Bangkok. That's where they sentenced us to death. We were not surprised. But then: 'Our imperial leader has decided differently. Instead of the death sentence you will all get forced labor for the next twenty years.' Because, I think, the end of the war was already in sight.

Still, death was preferable to forced labor. Because I've done time in the Outram Road Jail in Singapore. Oh my God, oh my God, that was worse than hell itself. You were beaten all the time. My job was cleaning shit barrels or making reels for cables. There were almost 80 of us. Every so often, new idiots would be admitted, guys who had struck a Japanese soldier, for example. On average, about 10 men a day died there. Starvation and such. They just left you to croak there. Van Heemert died of hunger there.

I'd been in Outram Road for about three or four months, and then, all of a sudden, it was over, bang, just like that. The bomb had been dropped, and on August 15 I got out. I weighed 27 kilos at the time.

I'll tell you, the Japs misbehaved a lot, tried everything to break me. But when it was over, I said: 'What's done is done. You guys didn't do it for fun, either.' We got a bunch of those Japanese in Surabaya, and there they were kicked by the folks there. I said: 'Why are you doing that? Why didn't you do that sooner?' That I couldn't stand.

They wanted to give me the MWO.[4] One colonel told me: 'Thou art a brave man, indeed!' And: 'You have fought for the queen and the flag.' I said: "Me, fight for the queen? I've never seen her here. And for the flag? Do you really want to know what flag I looked at? That flag with that red ball in it! Because that's how I knew the Japanese were about. I was fighting for my life! That is all.' Then he said: 'For bravery and conduct then, and if not for loyalty, then surely for endurance.' They gave me the bronze cross for the time I fought in Burma: 'For courage, conduct, and endurance.' Courage I had for sure, there was conduct, too – for I survived – but loyal I was not! So I got a medal one rank below the other one, ha! The hell I care. As far as I'm concerned, you can toss it away.

After the war, all I did was look for danger, I was that anxious for something to happen. Why? I don't know. Walking about at night, there would be those idle loafers. I would head for them on purpose. I had this fine dagger. I had a revolver, too. My point of view is: It doesn't matter if you die. But I need a servant. So I've got to take somebody with me! I don't get it, either, when people fail to act whenever anyone gets beaten or raped out in the street. I am the first on the scene.

My daughters can do anything they please. They're free where I'm concerned. They go out at night, they have my permission, but I'll tell them how to defend themselves. One of them has a brown belt in judo.

Unfortunately, a month or so ago, I threw my revolver into the River Rhine. My wife, you see, she didn't approve. Neither did my children.

4   Militaire Willemsorde, the Netherlands' highest medal, for bravery, conduct and loyalty, and tantamount to a knighthood.

The police don't allow it, and my family kept on whining: 'You'll get into trouble with the law if you get caught.' But I've still got my *klewang*, my machete, here, underneath my bed. Often I jump out of bed, my heart thumping inside my head, thinking there is somebody there. I go straight for my weapon.

     I can't sleep without my klewang. Simply because I think I'll be attacked. I wake up whenever a door opens. I stay very alert. My hearing, everything I think and do, my entire life is still focused on that one thing. It's still not over where I'm concerned, it still haunts me. And I keep telling everyone: 'For God's sake, please don't just walk into my room at night, because I'm fast, I'm very fast, and that's when there's the risk of something happening.' It's just not something you can unlearn, the fear that they'll get there before you can. You've got to be fast, otherwise you're dead."

Willem Punt

"Barring a very few exceptions, not a native was seen jumping from the Junyo Maru." [1]

Born June 9, 1921 in Velzen, the Netherlands. Ended up as a seaman in the Dutch East Indies. The Japanese regarded him as a POW and shipped him to the Sumatra Railway to work as a forced laborer. The ship he was on, the Junyo Maru, was torpedoed. After the war, he became a ship's mate.

"When they smashed up Pearl Harbor, I was on leave in Surabaya. It all went damned fast after that. Pretty soon the Jap hordes moved in. First I ended up in camp Struiswijk, Batavia.[2] We had such loads of teaching materials in that prison that teachers and others who could instruct started asking themselves, hey, couldn't we just continue with life as usual and make ourselves useful? People were of the opinion that the war would only last five or six months. They were determined to make good use of their time. So they started up a junior high, a high school, all sorts of things. Also a maritime academy. Therefore, I could go to school. I have a studious nature. And I also wanted to be noticed a bit by other people who now got to know me. The reason is that they were guys with initiative, all of them directors of things. I wanted to show those men that Willem Punt wasn't just anybody. My stay in Struiswijk prison lasted about two years. So I had two years of school. There came a moment when I was close to graduating, while things were not going well for the Japs, and I thought: No, guys, let's not have peace just yet, okay, for I'm not ready yet. What a rotten thing to think! Very negative, don't you think? You can imagine how preoccupied I was, that whole prison didn't even exist for me. Only my studies, my future, and impressing people mattered. They transferred us to the camp in Bandung, and there we continued with business as usual. We just had different instructors. In that Bandung camp, there were a lot of naval officers who routinely had served on examination committees. So that's where I took my exam for third mate. I graduated, cum laude.

Then they shipped us elsewhere. When we arrived and got off the train, we found ourselves in Tanjung Priok. This meant that we'd be shipped overseas. It appears that the Junyo Maru was waiting for us, not that I knew its name at the time, it didn't even bear a name. Then I said to Leen Sloot, my buddy: 'Best let that mob embark before we do, let's go to the back of the line.' Because it's as hot as hell in a ship like that and there was, in addition, not enough room, so if at all possible you try to stay on deck. Thousands of native men went to the front end of the ship. I ended up on the rear end and then I saw that all the holds were crammed full of people. The Japs were beating them to get as many of them down into the holds. I moved aside a bit, I didn't want to go into that hold, and neither did Leen Sloot, and then they called for volunteers to stand close to the latrines. I volunteered. There were six of those latrines suspended from the railing, wooden boxes without a bottom but with just one slat to put your feet on. My job was to help people get into them and to keep the whole contraption clean. So I could stay on deck. Leen Sloot could not. He curled up in a structure where bales of rice lay stored. He never came out of there alive, by the way. So we were on our way, accompanied by two Jap escorts. Off Benkulu, at around 4:00 o'clock in the afternoon I think it must have been, there was a sudden explosion at midship. The engines stopped. A huge cloud of steam rose up and people called out: 'Don't be afraid, it's a boiler explosion.' Well, it turns out to have been a torpedo. And two seconds later another torpedo hit, right underneath my feet. Out of curiosity about the first explosion, I had walked to midship to see what the

---

1 See also the stories of Alex Bloem and Willem Wildeman.
2 Batavia is now Jakarta.

trouble was. That's when that torpedo struck, right underneath the latrines. My job as toilet lady definitely ended right there. There was a lot of panic among the guys down where the explosion had been. There was a lot of yelling and screaming, and those still capable of moving were trying to get out of that hold in any way possible. Along those narrow, wooden stairs. But people were trampling each other. Up on deck, there were stacks of life rafts with holding ropes around them, and these were tossed overboard without further ado. There were folks who got these rafts thrown onto their heads. There were people who jumped overboard without looking and they were right away sucked back inside because they had jumped right in front of that hole. The things people do in a panic, you know. I stood there watching in a bit of a stupid daze. I thought: This ship is sinking. So then I walked to the farthest point of the rear and I jumped overboard. That way the ship continued to move away from me. It was still in motion. I didn't want to be sucked into a sinking ship. Quite a lot of wreckage came floating up to the surface, and I pretty soon found myself a plank. And from that plank I could lie and observe how things went with that ship. It was a tragedy. Barring a very few exceptions, not a native was seen jumping from the Junyo Maru. They stayed on board. On the foredeck. They were all crying: 'Nippon, tolong!' Japan, help us. Yes, that's what they cried out. And they also started singing. Really mostly to attract attention. Well, the ship slid backwards, and at a certain moment it stood up on end and went down all at once. And that was the end of that. An odd sight. It was just as if I had been watching a movie, you can't believe you actually saw it.

Yes, that's when the water festivities started. I had my little plank, of course. But at night – it soon got dark – just imagine: Not a ship to be seen anymore, lots of people in the water, hundreds, thousands of them, but hardly visible. It even started to rain. I heard a lot of voices and I swam towards them, with my plank, and then I reached

a water tank from the Junyo Maru. It was occupied by a number of survivors. I, too, held onto that tank. They had a rotation system of sorts, so guys who got very tired could take turns lying up on that tank. But if you were up there, you were exposed to wind and rain. And if you're already half or completely naked that's as cold as hell. To get some rest anyway, we took to warming up one another a bit. We'd huddle close together. We looked like a bunch of gays. We did this till the next day. Every so often I'd notice somebody missing, and I think they must have drowned. I'm not sure, for I was in a bit of a trance, you see. The whole thing was a bit unreal. But we ended up floating among a whole bunch of Japs, who were also in the water, but armed. They had bayonets. We were surrounded. They wanted that tank. In the end, I just swam off, into the wild, blue yonder – so long, Willem. And after a while, I found myself really thinking: I'm curious to know when this party is going to end. That's when I saw a bale of sisal floating by, from that ship. I could climb on top of it, on my stomach, but with a sizeable wave I'd slide off again. I'd have to climb back up. Well, I must have done it 40 times or so, and the scouring cost me the skin on my chest. As I was perched on top of my little bale, I suddenly spotted a black object on the surface and I was hoping it would be a submarine. The one that had torpedoed us and maybe had come back to rescue us. I swam to it. I turned out to be an overturned lifeboat. I climbed onto it and I found myself on its bottom, high and dry. That's when I saw that I'd been wounded, my elbows and chest particularly. And my testicles were all swollen. They looked like a soccer ball. Because of irritation caused by the salt water. But I felt no pain and I managed to rest some. I was actually somewhat content with the way things were going.

That's when 14 Ambonese guys came towards me. While swimming, we turned the lifeboat right side up and baled it out. Finally, we could all 14 of us get into the sloop, and so we had a boat. All ot us were dry. It had a mast, and we also found a big rag that we could use for a sail. From my boat, I observed whole groups of survivors messing with life rafts. I steered the boat in their direction, because our sloop could easily hold 60 or 70 men. But the Ambonese forbade me to do so. I was made their prisoner more or less, and they sailed away. There was one Dutchman, who had left his group of survivors and who was now swimming into our direction. I hoisted him on board. Now there were two whites on board. There was one Ambonese, who spoke Dutch well, and he told me: 'Don't you meddle or say anything, for it will be the last thing you do. I'll protect you.' It got dark, we headed for the coast, and we continued, and the next day it got light again, and then I found that my white buddy was gone. I take it the Ambonese simply tossed him overboard...

After the war, I experienced a period when I actually felt a bit of self-pity. I had difficulty telling the story of the Junyo Maru. I can now, but not right after the war. I lacked the words to describe it all. The misery was still so very real. The odd thing is, and I blame myself a bit, when I lay in the water and experienced all of that, it didn't touch me all that much. But after the war it certainly bothered me. I could scarcely talk about it without starting to cry. But I slowly got over that. I think it had to do with my surroundings. Look, I came back to the Netherlands when the country was still down on its ass. And there wasn't a Dutchman who didn't have his own, sad tale to tell. And there were indeed stories quite a lot sadder than mine. But that's when I went to sea, after six months, and I really received good support from my colleagues. They simply let me talk. Just like you're doing with me now. And that really helps. With some exceptions, I gained perspective and left it behind some. Still, if anybody were to ask me: Come on, give us that yarn of the Junyo Maru, or about Leen Sloten, who was my buddy... Fellow student, too. Yes, and he drowned, goddammit, because he didn't want to do

what I wanted him to do. Maybe I wasn't aggressive enough in my dealings with him. I should have said: 'Come on, you'd better do as I say, we're in this together.' But I had the feeling that a certain distance had come between Leen and me. I was the guy who graduated cum laude, phew... whereas he had bombed. And there was that one time when I said: 'Your own fault, you should have worked harder.' And maybe I was going around boasting a bit. That's why I think: If only I had gone easier on him, maybe he would have come along.

Leen and I, we had a common acquaintance, an Orthodox Catholic priest. He was allowed to be married and he had children, too. Leen would take me along, and that priest would then celebrate mass in his own home in Batavia. I got along well with that family, and that's where I left my Dutch certificate of citizenship, my raincoat and some other clothes... Well, here we go again. Yes, yes...I got all of those things back on the Nieuw Amsterdam.[3] I met his wife there. With her kids... Well, as you can see, there's something bothering me. This is hitting close to home. I am really touched by the whole thing. I had quite a long conversation with that woman. My raincoat didn't fit me anymore, I left it there, for she could use it for the kids, but I still have my Dutch certificate of citizenship. Yes, that was a sad meeting. The priest had died. Leen had died. Isn't it weird, an entire ship sinks to the bottom of the sea, and for that I don't shed a tear.

To put it in fancy language a bit, I think the war has had a purifying effect on me rather than a depressing effect. I'm from a Christian Reformed family and, therefore, reared in fear of the Lord. There's not much of that left, by the way. It meant, though, that when I went to sea I was really afraid of most things. The way I was raised made me fearful, for I truly believed in fire and brimstone. Also, that God took care of you but also freely punished you. You could say that was something I learned not

3   The ship on which he returned to the Netherlands.

to believe in anymore during the war. I began to see the relative value of things. Moreover, it pretty soon dawned on me that the faith I was indoctrinated with is in fact worthless. That is not to say that I don't believe in anything, no, I believe in nature. With a capital N, of course. But not those Bible stories. And not all that scary stuff, the kind they feed you in those Christian churches. They tell you that God hears our prayers. Well, there has certainly been a great deal of prayer. Doesn't help one bit. On that boat, you know, just on that Junyo Maru, people prayed as if their lives depended on it. Led by ministers, priests, and other faithful denizens. And I also heard those Muslims pray and sing to Allah, the whole bunch of them. Didn't help a bit. They all drowned."

Frank Salden

"The ability to truly delight in things is, really, something I lost because of the war."

Born May 1, 1924, in Yogyakarta, Java. He was just 17 years old when he enlisted as a volunteer in the KNIL, the army of the Dutch East Indies. During the war, he did forced labor building airfields on the island of Flores; he then worked on the Sumatra Railway. He became a physician after the war.

"On Flores I nearly died of malaria and beriberi. We were there for about a year, from 1943 till 1944. Quite a lot of working parties were taken there to make airfields, two or three even. They were intended for the attack on Australia. Fortunately, it never came to that. The toll there was actually quite a lot less than the toll on Sumatra – the death toll, I mean. The population on Flores helped us a lot with food, and I actually owe my life to that, too. Because I was in bad shape due to that beri-beri, until the local people provided us with *katjang idju*, a small green pea very rich in vitamin B. That's what cured me.

After Flores, I ended up in Batavia,[1] in the Xth Battalion.[2] From there, several transports left for Sumatra. Mine first landed at Singapore, where we spent some time in the River Valley Camp, a very bad place. From there we went across to Pekanbaru in a very small ship, the old ferry Elizabeth.

We were very happy to return from Flores to Java and be back on native soil, so to speak. But we got a real fright when they took us away again, and we ended up in the real Sumatran jungle. The area around Pekanbaru and along the railway was still a primeval forest. That entire region I've always considered very eerie, very frightening.

1   Now called Jakarta.

2   The name of the barracks.

And very depressing, too, was its primitive housing, the bad food, the hunger, and increasingly being confronted with people so ill that they died on the spot or were taken to camp number 2, which was the end of the line for a whole lot of people. As the railway line got further south, the Japanese increasingly got into more of a hurry. They became more nervous all the time, the beatings and the frenzy got worse, and we were forced to work increasingly longer hours. During the final month or so, we'd leave before sunup and didn't return to camp till well after sundown. We worked incredibly long days.

I've seen a lot of camps, always in a group of people building the railway. We'd carry rails, carry railroad ties, we'd be driving in nails, and all that sort of work I've had to do at one time or another. I've not been sick much along the railway. All I got were tropical sores, huge, big sores I've had. But you could work with those, they were never that bad. I was hungry a lot, though.

I returned to the Netherlands toward the end of 1946, discharged from the army because of, shall we say, depression and decreased powers of concentration. I right away started on my college education. Before the war I'd been planning to go into civil engineering. I thought it'd be great to construct bridges and irrigation works and that sort of thing. The war caused me to change my mind because of the misery I saw around me then. Before the war I was a superficial man who enjoyed life. After the war I was an idealist, and very serious. I studied medicine with the intention of going back to Indonesia and help alleviate its misery. That didn't work since the Indonesians didn't allow me to return because of my service in the colonial army. Instead, I ended up in Africa, where I worked as a doctor for almost eight years.

From 1946 until 1976, I never spent a moment thinking about my time in the prison camp. I had totally forgotten about it, banned it totally from memory. In 1976, I began to suffer from hypertension. I was increasingly disturbed by dreams and nightmares. Sometimes my experiences in Indonesia would feature in them, but they were mostly completely absurd nightmares that didn't relate to anything. The second thing that happened was that I could hardly concentrate on anything anymore and I became increasingly convinced that I was becoming demented. The latter I considered worse than anything. I had a theory about it: I suffered from lack of vitamins, and that has a deleterious effect on both the brain and the nervous system. We do know that pellagra causes dementia. So I ascribed all of this to my camp experiences. With hindsight, I can say that I was wrong, for I didn't become demented.

A psychiatrist advised me to take off from work for three months and take a big trip. My question then was, would a trip to Indonesia be the thing to do? They thought that was a sound idea. It actually turned out to be quite a nice trip. But to enjoy things – one of the effects of this war is that I have lost the ability truly to delight in things. There are things I find beautiful or impressive, I'm fond of my grandchildren, I can spend hours with them, but I can't really delight in things anymore. Beside that, I've got to admit that the trip was beautiful. But I traveled alone and I found that increasingly uncomfortable. There was nobody I could really talk with about my experiences. In those days, I kept a diary written in a letter format, four to five pages a day, which I read again later on. Then I noticed that I became increasingly somber. That wasn't something I was fully aware of. It only became evident when I got back to the Netherlands. But I returned totally overwrought.

After that, after I tried to take my own life twice, they treated me for depression in a psychiatric institution. A Professor Bastiaans,[2] who developed the notion of the POW syndrome, treated my psychic ailment. He was the one who also diagnosed me as such. This psychiatric treatment did wonders for me, but at the same time I developed an obsession. I wanted to know everything there was to know about the colonial army, about the Dutch East Indies and its history. I've since amassed an impressive library. Ever since that trip, I've actually been preoccupied with the Indies and with what is now called Indonesia.

Now those nightmares are much less serious and much more rare, you know, just incidental. True, I always wake up early, between five and six. And my last dream is never what you might call an enjoyable dream, but still not quite what you might call a nightmare. You could just call it a lousy dream, nothing else. I've got to tell you, though, ever since your phone call a few days ago, a whole lot of memories have come to the surface and I've not been sleeping as well again. I'll thank the Lord on my knees when this conversation is over.

What I've ended up with is a perpetual lack of enthusiasm. At parties I just sit there, well, not really participating. I'm not really depressed but I simply lack the ability to enjoy things, I don't initiate much of anything, I'm a bit of an outsider where my social contacts are concerned, and I don't really have friends anymore. Beyond that, well, I read a great deal and I study a lot. After the war ended, when we were still in Sumatra, the English served us whiskey. I've actually been drinking quite a lot ever since. I don't drink during the day, you know. I don't start until after 10:00 o'clock at night. After a few glasses of whiskey I find life a lot easier."

2   Also see the stories of De Bruïne and Muller.

Henk Wiersma

"The thing that haunts me is hatred, pure and simple!"

Born September 21, 1918, in Engwierum, the Netherlands. During the Great Depression, he enlisted as a soldier and left for the Dutch East Indies. In October 1942, now as a POW, he was transported by ship and forced to work on the Burma Railway. After the war, he became a professional soldier in the Royal Netherlands Army. He died on November 13, 2004.

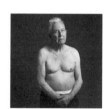

"When the war broke out, I was stationed in Batavia[1] on the island of Java. I'd gotten married there in 1940, my wife was native-born. I never saw the enemy till we surrendered. After some time, I was interned in the Xth Battalion[2] in Batavia. From there we headed for Burma. We went on board the Tacoma Maru,[3] that's what the ship was called, in Tanjung Priok, Batavia's harbor. They herded us in with their rifle butts, about 1,600 or 1,700 of us. During the voyage, we were attacked by American submarines. Our ship fled and anchored in a bay close to Moulmein.

We must have stayed there, in that terrible heat, for about nine or ten days, and a lot of people died there. Dysentery is what did them in. There was hardly anything to eat. I, too, started to get feeble. After that, we ended up in Moulmein's town prison. And again a lot of people died. From there, we went to Thanbyuzayat. That's where I first got health problems. Because of a vitamin deficiency I could no longer see well and I ended up with a case of total night blindness.

After a while things got a little better. Then I was put to work, first in Retpu, later on in camp 108, near the Three Pagoda Pass, close to the Thai border. I worked there for a long time and they really beat the hell out of us. We were severely maltreated. The Japs were not so bad, actually, they were mostly there to build the railroad. The Koreans, however, who were our actual guards working for the Japanese, those turned out to be the real racists, those were the real bastards. They were true brutes. I still remember their names. There was 'The Beard,' that's what we called the commander of camp 108, and then there was 'Rubber Lips.' They tried to humiliate you in all sorts of ways and they would kick and beat the hell out of you. 'The Beard' was executed by firing squad after the war.

After the railroad was finished, I was made to cut wood. Wood to fuel the train engines. And later on, probably toward the end of 1943, or early in 1944, they took us somewhere else. We were meant to go to Japan, but we got no farther than Saigon. That's where I worked on the docks, loading and unloading ships. But our principal task was working on their airports. Also very hard work. After that was done more or less, they stashed us onto a ship to take us away. We headed up the Mekong River and at some stage we thought we were going to die for sure. But then the atom bombs dropped. So then we went back to Saigon, where they liberated us. I was really malnourished and I spent a couple of months in the hospital, where I got back on my feet a bit. But I continued to suffer from night blindness. That took a very long time indeed.

I can never quite get over it, working on that railroad. Not that I think about it all day, no, that wouldn't be good. But now and then it all comes back to me, sure enough. And especially at night, that's when I get things such as nightmares, not that I have them anymore, you know, that's over with. Among other things, I still dream a lot about those times, but those aren't nightmares as such. For sure, I do dream about being punished and maltreated. And all that lifting and carrying

1 Now Jakarta.

2 The name of the barracks.

3 See also the story of Chris Moonen.

huge loads, on and on, without end. I can still see myself with that pickax, that was the hardest job. You had to chip away at that *karang*, loosen that hard rock. And then there was that terrible weather. I think they get more rain than anywhere else in the world. But still, we always had to keep working. That we did virtually naked, really, all I had on was a *tjawat*, a small loincloth just in front, and no more. And after the war I spent time in Singapore, where we did guard duty in Changi Jail. That's where they hanged those Japanese or Koreans I mentioned. That's another thing you can never forget, you know. The Americans served them a last meal, and of course I don't think they deserved it.

This has also got to do with the missus, of course, who was awfully mistreated. They beat her unconscious, and she landed in prison. That was still in the city of Batavia, where she managed to live outside of the internment camps. She shouldn't have, but she did anyway. She passed a Korean who was on guard. She was supposed to bow but didn't. And so he beat her unconscious. Back in the Netherlands, she had to undergo quite a number of operations to her head.

Once in Holland, all this caused her a lot of problems, and then all that stuff surfaced with me again, too. Well, it's your wife, of course, and that makes it extra bad. She had many nightmares and cried a lot. In the beginning, in the 1950s, things were at their worst. I had trouble on the job because these things never left you. For 17 years I was in the army. Later on, these things faded into the background some, and life improved. That was around the mid-50s. I had no time to think. Fact is, I tried to make something of myself here. You came back to Holland and had to start all over again. So I went off to school, studying to make sergeant. Then to school for sergeant-major. That took a lot of effort. And then, you know, those memories about the war tend to fade, and they no longer trouble you as much. However, the moment the wife got problems with her health again, then that would affect me, too.

Later the wife really started ailing. That lasted many years. In the 1990s, it got really bad. She was totally emaciated by then, all worn out. During the war, she went hungry all the time and what little she had she gave to her child. She was just skin and bones, a skeleton, really. And when you get older that has a real impact, you know. She was little more than a frail ghost when you saw her. Her memory was all shot and she was totally demented. And she would be talking only about the Japanese occupation. She used to lay here on the couch a lot, and she died at home, too. That's when it all surfaced with me again, too. Those goddamned Koreans.

You're not supposed to keep on hating. Then again, take someone like Dolf Winkler.[4] He went to Japan and talked to those brutes and people like that – well, I just don't know. I couldn't do that. Even now, I can't stand the sight of a Korean. You should know that I also sing in the church choir. The director came up with a Christmas song, a Korean Christmas song it was. She handed it out. I walked right out, that's how shocked I was. I told her: "This thing?! I'm not singing anything of the sort. Those brutes, what were you thinking?" I told her: "I'm quitting, I don't want to sing here anymore." Well, they put it away and never mentioned it again. It wasn't their fault, after all.

Then, too, we've got a Korean child living in our village here. Someone adopted it. Imagine, in a town as small as this! I was taken aback when all of a sudden I saw that Korean here. Well, not at first, of course, then it was still small. Now, however, he must be around 16, or maybe as old as 18 already, I guess. That's when you recognize those brutes in a kid like that. Whenever I see that boy, everything comes back to me. I could easily kill him, just like that. It's not his fault, of course, it's a child from a different era, after all, but still,

4   See also the story of Dolf Winkler.

the thing that consumes me is hatred, pure and simple! It's wrong, it's not the Christian thing to do. I should forget it, really. But it happens, just like that. That makes it so difficult. I've been thinking, I really ought to have a talk with the boy's parents one of these days, but I haven't been able yet to gather enough courage to do so."

Willem Wildeman

"I still can't stand the sight of a Japanese."

Born September 26, 1915, in Hendrik-Ido-
Ambacht, the Netherlands. He was a sailor before
the war. Overtaken by events in the Indies,
the Japanese regarded him as a POW.
They shipped him to the Sumatra Railway on
board the Junyo Maru,[1] which was torpedoed.
After the war, he worked as a bench fitter and
a teacher in South Africa. He's been living in
the Netherlands since 1993.

"I studied to be a ship's engineer. On December
7, our ship was in Honolulu and we got our share
of the Pearl Harbor bombardment. In August or
September of 1942, the Japanese picked me up off
the streets in Bandung. First I was interned in a
camp for civilians. But I had served in the merchant
marine, and according to Japanese law, the merchant navy is part of the military. So they removed
me from that camp and put me into a prison camp
for soldiers in Batavia.[2]

Our trip began on a certain day in September
1944, in the middle of the night. To Tanjung Priok.
That's where the Junyo Maru was berthed. It was
a small ship, you know. But it turned into one big
hell for in some places you couldn't even stand.
There were 2,400 of us just on the afterdeck, while
the foredeck held 4,000 romushas. We knew how
to organize ourselves, while those poor romushas
didn't know what organization was. It must have
been sheer hell for those poor men. We had two
days of that. The food was good, fortunately, and
we didn't go hungry. I didn't go thirsty, either,
unlike a lot of other people on the ship, you know.
And then, around 4:00 in the afternoon, there was
a big bang, and two minutes later another bang,
and then we knew what was happening. What, in

hindsight, probably saved my life was that I didn't
jump overboard immediately. I was a sailor, after
all, and so I knew that either the ship would sink
within 10 seconds, or that it would remain afloat
for quite some time. So I stayed up on deck
until the water got about that far from the deck.
The ship's stern was already submerged when
I said to myself: Okay, Willem, now it's time to
jump. That jump, toward your death, has caused
me to have nightmares for years. Because you
knew: This is the end.

First I looked to see how the ship would
sink. That's when I noticed that at least some
3,000 romushas were still on the foredeck. So we
saw them go down with the ship. For the rest of my
life I'll not forget that enormous scream coming
from the throats of those 3,000 young men. That
scream wasn't loud so much as intense. It was an
intense death's scream from 3,000 romushas. Well,
when that was over and done with, it was time
to survey the scene. You didn't really know what
to do. Until I spotted a small ship quite far away.
I swam towards it. I don't know for how long I
was swimming. But it took a long time. That small
ship took me to Sumatra.

I'll tell you this: If I had to choose between
the Junyo Maru getting torpedoed and the bombing of Pearl Harbor, then being torpedoed is the
most important moment in my life. That bombing
everybody is talking about really didn't mean much
to me. I just stood there looking at those planes,
watching the bombs drop, but I didn't realize then
that my life was in danger. But on the Junyo Maru
I did. That was true misery, you understand. When
you see all those corpses floating by, with a few
people swimming, then you realize that the chance
of rescue, of yours truly included, is close to zero.
That's really been the cause of my nightmares.
I had those for years on end. Then one day I lay
down in bed and wondered why those nightmares
kept coming back. That's when I did some constructive thinking: How jumping into the sea was

1   See also the stories of Alex Bloem and Willem Punt.

2   Now Jakarta.

tantamount to jumping to one's death. And that swimming, that great outcry, that's when I fully realized what had happened, and that's when the nightmares mostly disappeared. They recur every so often, once or twice a year, but it's not that bad. I myself have talked them out of my own head. Or, to put it differently: given them a place of their own in my soul.

In addition, when I returned to the Netherlands, I was naturally full of stories about Indonesia. On the first day, when I woke up, I went downstairs and found that my father had already gone to work. My stepmother sat at the table, it must have been around 8:00 o'clock. I started to talk with her about Indonesia. I continued doing that every day for at least a week, and that's how I unburdened my memory through talking, knowing full well that the poor dear wouldn't remember a thing, for she was suffering from dementia. However, I had talked the whole thing away, as it were. It was out of my system. I was done.

I couldn't work then. I was simply too weak. But I did see one thing clearly, that the Netherlands were finished, had gotten old and messy, while I was young, wanting to get ahead, and I wanted to see changes. That's when my father said to me: "Willy, you've got to go, you should emigrate." That made quite an impact. America, that's not where I wanted to go; that's fine when you're 16, otherwise you're too old. Canada was too cold. Australia, that was warmer, but I had met Australians, and they were not the sort of people I wanted to deal with. New Zealand was practically impossible for people who didn't speak English. So that left South Africa. I went to Pretoria, I got work there, and I stayed there for 45 years.

Look, in Indonesia I didn't have any family or friends. Making friends in the prison camp was very difficult. Oh yes, if you knew a thing or two about plants, for example, that was useful. But I didn't. So, talking of friendships... I was terribly lonely. All alone in all of Indonesia. It has its advantages, because I wasn't out to make friends. I was only aiming for one thing: Passing time. I've got to get through this. And if that atomic bomb had fallen one week later, I would not have been here. Sure thing.

They sent me to camp number 2, the death camp, and that's where I stayed for a couple of months. I've had everything, all the prison camp diseases. Take dysentery, for 10 or 15 years at least I still felt death lurking here. I've got a granddaughter who's three years old. I don't want her to kiss me. I've got so many nasty diseases in me, I just don't want to expose the little girl to even the slightest risk of catching something from me.

And then those beatings: I got a couple of hard blows a couple of times and my eardrums cracked. For three weeks I was as deaf as a post. Well, that same ear is still functioning at 65 percent.

Have I ever seen people being beaten later on? In South Africa, when I was still a bench fitter, there was one black man who was invariably loafing around. One day, the foreman, who was the boss there, got this guy into his office and gave him a terrible beating. He never had another problem with that black guy. It's the only thing they understand. I'm not a racist, but I don't care at all for other races, for those black and colored people. Not even in South Africa. Maybe that has something to do with the Japanese as well. I don't know. The cause may originate from the prison camp days. Because I didn't use to be like that.

I still can't stand the sight of a Japanese. Whenever I see one in a photograph, I think that bastard, that rotten Jap. Ah, but I do own a Japanese car. But not because I love Japan all that much. Toyotas are very good cars. And I don't see why I should shortchange myself because of my anti-Japanese sentiments. But I still feel a bit guilty for having bought one."

Dolf Winkler

"That war will continue for as long as we live."

Born April 8, 1917, in Amsterdam. In 1940, he went to the Dutch East Indies as a soldier to escape unemployment during the Great Depression. As a POW, he worked first on the Burma Railway, then in a coalmine in Japan.
After the war, he was, among other things, an interior decorator, designer, entrepreneur, and council member of the city of Emmeloord, the Netherlands, representing the Labor Party. He also held various management jobs.

"Following our surrender, we had to bury the people who'd been killed in the fortifications at Ciater.[1] There, 72 men had been shot dead, and their bodies were still lying about. All you had to do was follow your nose; their bodies were practically decomposed. We had to dig a deep pit, but the stench was unbearable, with the bodies almost falling apart. The next day, our commanding officer got us some cologne to make the air a bit more bearable.

Then we went to Cilacap. We were left standing on our feet for over 24 hours. They wanted us to sign a form stating that we'd obey the Japanese code of military conduct and that we'd not attempt to escape. Our Dutch commanding officers told us not to sign. The result was that we all got a terrible beating. In our army, it is customary to stand at ease with your hands folded behind your back. Not so in the Japanese army, where they hold their hands down along their sides. I didn't know about that. At some stage this one Japanese guy sneaked up on me from behind. Using his leather army belt, he beat me up severely, my eyes nearly popping from their sockets, as it were. I'm reminded of this whenever I tighten my belt.

After a while, we went to Batavia[2] and from there by ship to Singapore. From there, packed like sardines, we went by train to Thailand.

The wagons were made of corrugated iron, hotter than hell during the day and icy cold at night. Five days and five nights we had of this. Then we arrived in Banpong, and from there we had to go to Kinsayok. That turned out to be an almost 30-mile walk. There were guys who simply couldn't hack it and they just dropped dead alongside the road, exhausted. It was cold, we didn't possess a thing, just a small bag with a few things, like some snapshots you wanted to salvage. We slept alongside the road. Fortunately, this was during the dry monsoon. When we finally arrived, we still had to construct our own barracks, using bamboo. We were not familiar with this, and the whole thing was so flimsily built that the mosquitoes zipped right through it. I, too, got a good dose of malaria, with a burning fever and cold shivers. My buddies carried me to the side and put me close to the forest, in the shade and away from the job. I'll never forget how that rotten Jap, whom we called 'Horse Face,' spotted me lying there and beat me up. When he was through, he threw me into the *kali*, the river, where I 'could cool off.'

I ended up in the sickbay with doctor Van der Meulen, a man with a great deal of experience in tropical medicine. He asked me to assist him, showed me the ropes a bit, and so, for a few weeks, I walked around as a male nurse. One of the things I had to do was scrape and clean out tropical sores. That was something horrendous. The patient would be held down by force, while I had to scrape the wound clean with a spoon. Van der Meulen also experimented using maggots, instead. That way, a lot of the guys got to keep their legs. The English doctors used to amputate. But this guy put maggots onto the sores, which they ate clean. Unfortunately, the doctor later died of cholera.

After the railway was done in October of 1943, we all had a medical check-up. And I belonged to the so-called fit men. These were taken to

1   See also the story of Ben de Lizer.
2   Now Jakarta.

Singapore first, and then shipped out to Japan in old, rotten boats. Five ships in all. Three of them were torpedoed. Several thousand boys lost their lives that way.

In Japan, in the town of Mizumaki, we were put to work in their coalmines. That was a real nightmare, far scarier than the whole Burma Railroad thing had been. There, at least, we had worked out in the open. Down in the mine, however, everything was dark, and then there was the ever-present fear of collapse. We had to work in shafts with supports at every five or six yards only, whereas Dutch coalmines have supports at every yard, at least. It was all slate, very brittle and extremely dangerous. I handled the drill, so I was up front. So there came a moment when everything behind me went 'whap,' and the three of us found ourselves cut off. When our batteries were dead, we couldn't see a hand in front of our eyes anymore. I started beating myself on the head and pressing my fingernails into my own body. Nobody said a thing till someone started to scream, another began to pray, and I started to swear. We were beside ourselves with fear. We were very lucky that oxygen seeped through the cracks.

For years, I've walked around with the memory of that collapse, which trapped us for several days. I'll never quite get over it. It's not that I'm afraid of going into a basement or something like that, I'm over that now, but there are things you see on TV that remind you of it. I personally don't have psychological problems anymore. On the other hand, I still say that that war will continue for as long as we live.

During the first couple of years following the war, I walked around with a great deal of anger and resentment. Since 1970, I've visited Indonesia three or four times, together with my wife, who's not from the Indies. And I've been to Thailand with her, where I've relived everything. That's were I first was confronted with the graves of friends, alongside the railroad, and that was a bit of a downer. I felt guilty. They were dead, and I wasn't. A funny feeling.

I still had my own business then, Winkler's Furniture, employing 35 people. To forget about the war, a lot of people sought their refuge in pushing themselves, in working hard, myself included. Take, for example, the times I had to drive down to Keierbach in southern Germany. I'd leave at 3:00 in the morning in a fast Mercedes, and I'd be back that same night. That meant I had driven some 700 miles. Crazy. You still felt yourself pursued by the Japanese, still hounded, as it were. So the time came when I just could not go on anymore. I'd been working too hard, and I was spent.

In 1976, I was for half a year in the care of Bastiaans,[3] the psychiatrist, who told me – we were on a first-name basis – 'Listen, Dolf, there are so many things you can do, now go and do something else.' He's the one who put me on the right track. That's when I put an ad in the paper, sold my business and started visiting people. I made recordings on tape of all our conversations. I collected all sorts of materials, which I donated to the Museon, the museum of education in The Hague. In 1980, they asked me to put together an exhibition. I entered politics and became the provincial president of the ANBO, an interest group for the elderly. I became a member of the city council representing the Labor Party and I was on the board of the SWO, a foundation assisting the elderly. I became advisor to a housing corporation. In short, I've done all sorts of things, but all of them worthwhile, enjoyable things.

During the war in the Mizumaki coalmine, I met Tamura. He was a Japanese man who took pity on us. He, too, was forced to work in the coalmines. He was a supervisor there, although his real profession was something quite different. He was a very humane person, who often gave us a rest break. He never beat us. Of the little food he had he shared with us some small fish. He also looked after me during a spell of malaria. That man has never been

3   See also Han de Bruïne and Ko Muller.

out of my thoughts. He set me to thinking that there must have been more Japanese who were indeed good people. So one day I told my wife: You know what? I'd like to go to Japan and visit the coalmine where I worked. And I want to try and meet that man Tamura again.

Off to Japan we went, in 1985 that was. The train took us as far as Fukuoka, some 40 miles from the city of Mizumaki. The little station was exactly as I remembered it, but I could no longer find the road leading to our camp for everything was paved over and such. So I said: Let's go to the police station and ask there. Well, the policeman in charge thought the whole thing very odd, for the town is hardly a tourist spot. However, I do speak a bit of broken Japanese and I managed to make myself understood. The man called an official at city hall, I got on the phone, they ordered a cab, and that's how I ended up at the coalmines' office. They received us like royalty, they served tea and what have you, and then we visited the mines and the camp. The next day our hotel was overrun by television crews and journalists, who all interviewed me. At the site of the camp, they made a documentary about me. That's where I saw memorials dedicated to Japanese men who had died in the coalmines, and then I asked them: Isn't there any memorial for us? That's when a journalist took me over to a small, mossy cross.

There had been a time when two Australian prisoners had escaped from camp. They had been caught and shot to death by firing squad. After the war, several Australian judges came over to try the war criminals. The Japanese then quickly put up a niche with a small cross on top dedicated to POWs who had died there. I think they did it to elude prosecution.

I told them: Is this all there is? I find this an outrage. I'm going to tell people about this. Anyway, I got to talk to the mayor of Mizumaki, I wrote the Dutch ambassador to Japan and I wrote the Ministry of Foreign Affairs to get this monument restored. Foreign affairs subsequently told us that the

monument had been cleaned up. I told my wife: You know what? I'm off to Japan again. I want to turn this into something. I had to pay for the whole thing myself, you know. Sure, it had been cleaned, but oh boy, the whole thing was broken down, and that's when I started making some demands. I proposed listing on the monument the names of all 53 boys who had died, all men from that coalmining camp, camp number 6. That's what happened. And that's when I said: 'That's not enough, I want to see it made into an even bigger monument, one with wings added to it, bearing the name of every Dutchman who died in Japan.' 'Yes, Mr. Winkler, but those people didn't die here, not in our town. We'd like to help you, but not at our expense.' Well, sure, I could see their point, and so I got things rolling, back in the Netherlands. That's when I received some money from the Ministry of Foreign Affairs. I've spent days with the people from the war graves commission, all those names had to be traced, but in short, we saw the whole project through. And that's how the monument came to be fine and finished in the end.

In one of the TV broadcasts, I had said that I wished to meet Tamura, that good Japanese man. The next day, his daughter-in-law called me up to say he was still alive. They organized everything for us; he lived some 375 miles away somewhere. The whole village came to meet us. It did me a world of good how nicely those people treated me, people who had their own share of guilt. Sure, the Japanese have that too, you know, guilt about their parents' misdeeds. Anyway, that inspired me to continue, despite the threats I got at first. There was quite a lot of consternation among a lot of people who said: 'You are a Jap lover!' They made death threats to me over the phone, saying: 'I know where to find you.' I find the whole thing pitiful. Walking around with feelings of hatred all your life, that just isn't healthy, you know. A culture of victimization often is still prevalent within Indies communities. Those are people unable to break out of what's in fact a vicious circle.

Of course, you can't forget the war, but there comes a time when you have to put a period behind it all. My feelings of hatred have altogether disappeared because of my trips to Japan, meeting its youth, the present generation of Japanese, whom you simply can't hold accountable for the misdeeds of the previous generation. When I was a member of the Emmeloord city council, I fought for and got money to establish a youth exchange program. Every year now, there's an exchange between the children here and children in Japan, and they've established a club called 'The Friends of Japan.' That's a good thing right there.

I've established a foundation called EKNJ for former POWs in Japan and their descendants. We've published three books in Japan. We provide information to schools. Together with the Museon here, I organized an exhibit in Osaka, Japan. Thousands of schoolchildren have been to see it. We tell what happened and about the bad things that were done. But I also tell them about the things we, the Dutch, did in Indonesia before the war. About the shenanigans of Mr. Van Heutz and Mr. Daendels and Mr. Westerling,[4] and the thousands of Indonesians killed. We occupied the Indies for 400 years. We've done good things but bad things as well.

We've managed to see to it that schools in Japan take weekly turns cleaning the monument. At the time, we were thinking of giving them a high-pressure cleaner. 'No,' one of their teachers told us, 'they've got to use their hands, because they have to feel what has happened.' During a memorial service those children sing the Dutch national anthem. By now, they know the lyrics better than we do.

Those people have become my friends. The mayor of Mizumaki has been to visit me. I was the first former POW to give a speech in Hiroshima, a speech that was broadcast by radio. And after meeting Tamura again, I started thinking: 'I'd like to involve others in the things I've been through.' That is why I've been to visit Japan with other former POWs. Increasingly, more people joined me, close to 300 by now. And those same people returned cured, as it were, healed, just like me. I'm so glad that they, too, feel liberated."

4   They were, respectively, a notorious Dutch general during colonial wars in Aceh; a governor-general who built a road across Java at the expense of many Indonesian lives; and a soldier turned mercenary during the Indonesian war of independence.

George Voorneman

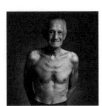

"If you are cruel you shall be punished."

Born July 12, 1920, in Bandung. Was made a
POW and ended up as a forced laborer on the
Burma Railway line.
After the war, he first joined the Dutch and then
the Indonesian navy. He lived in Jakarta, previous-
ly called Batavia, where he died April 17, 2005.

"Sad to say, what my mother told me then is still
true today: 'Son, you've got a birthmark close to
your eye. For as long as you live, you'll cry and
you'll always have headaches.' That proved to be
true. I lost my eye. That's not an eye right there
above that birthmark, that's a prosthesis. But how
did I come to have a lost eye?

I was drafted into the navy in 1939.
Something I'm very proud of. That made me the
youngest corporal ever since Michiel Adriaenszoon
de Ruyter[1] hundreds of years ago. Age 20. During
the fight at the Wonokromoh Bridge in Surabaya,
with the Japanese on the other side, I get this
splinter in my eye. Never mind, I fight on, fighting
for my country. Two days later, I get operated on.
I lie in the hospital a month, a month and a half.
I get a porcelain eye; plastic does not exist yet.
Do you want to see my eye? Rather not, eh? And
a nurse, she, too, tells me: 'Son, for as long as
you live you'll have headaches.' Because of my
eye. For sure, I always have my headaches. Quite
a bother, you know.

Then a bunch of Japanese came to get me.
That's when my life as a POW begins. They sent me
to Batavia, then to Singapore, and then by train
in four days and three nights to Siam.[2] And in that
place Banpong, I find it very pretty, at first. The
Siamese treat us to bananas. And from that spot
they send us into the jungle by truck. That's where
the misery starts, yes, on that railroad, where I get
to know every disease. I get to Burma, on the border, but there I fall ill. They send me back again.

That's where I stay, in Nakhom Pathon. Till liberation. In the big hospital, with various doctors
and surgeons and stuff like that. But stuff to
operate with? A pal of mine, a Dutch boy, he gets
a skull operation. They just use a chisel, believe
it or not. And a carpenter's saw, for wood and
furniture, such stuff.

I have a different disease: My eye. And my
eye means my remaining eye. It's getting worse
for lack of vitamins. I've been blind. I carry this
rope with a small wooden board with Japanese
characters on it. You have to make a bow to every
Japanese you meet, you know, like a jackknife.
And because I am blind I don't have to.

And a lucky thing it is that God is always
helping me. There are many boys who are hopeless.
I tell them:

> 'A mighty fortress is our God,
> A bulwark never failing;
> Our helper He amid the flood
> Of mortal ills prevailing.
> He smites His enemies and foes,
> Armored with fear and lying,
> Like chaff He sends them flying.'[3]

And indeed, they will fly off like chaff.

The Korean guys in those days were serving
the Japanese. One Korean was a sadist, a bit too
much. 'Jungle Jim' we call him. But if you are cruel,
you shall be punished. Following liberation, the
Koreans in Nakhom Pathon are our prisoners.
They were free to walk around some and we allowed
them to go into town. Nakhom Pathon has the
tallest temple in the whole world, a pagoda of
about 200 yards. That Jungle Jim fellow, he lets
himself fall from the very top, and at that moment
he croaks, of course, you see? Suicide. Because
of his sins, of course.

---

1   Famous 17th century Dutch admiral.

2   Former name of Thailand.

In 1946, I'm off for the Netherlands. The navy reception center in the town of Doorn takes me in. My eye is my handicap. My left eye, that is, because the other is dead already and can't be fixed. You want to see? Let me show you, so you'll know what I'm talking about. Look at that!

They send me all over the place. To the city of Utrecht, where I walked from the station all the way to the *Oog in Al* neighborhood, where the eye clinic was. The whole trip. God, where am I, that's what I'm thinking. The eye's no good because of malnutrition in the prison camp. But in Holland they feed me well. I live like a king. They don't find anything wrong with that eye. It's just bad. Then it gets better, the food, you know. The thing to do is eat orange stuff, carrots and things like that. That's proper eye medicine.

Still in 1946, in December, they sent me back. When I arrived, I went to see the doctor in Batavia. For my eye and such, to get compensation. 'No way, my boy,' this doctor says, 'you've got to go back to Holland.' That's how they sent me from one place to another. And look here, man, that doctor fellow belongs to my own race, an Indies fellow.

However, I stay here, for my mother. She had six children. Those six, all gone. A couple of them got butchered. One of them in Ambarawa, the civilian internment camp near Semarang on Java. And one of them caused my mother to get her gray hair all at once, because he was so badly treated by one of her own race, a Javanese. Was taken to Jakarta and died here. Well, I don't have the heart to leave my mother behind, a woman who has nothing. So I see to it she gets something to eat. I love my mother. Even though she's illiterate, she's my mother.

In 1948 I got that kind of badge saying I'd fought for queen and country, and from the admiral another, for law and order. But with that one eye – look here, I was supposed to make officer. Alas, impossible. You can't be a one-eyed man in the military, that's not going to happen. If I could see, I'd have made general way back when. However, the only thing I have to look for money with, for my kids, is just that one eye. I asked for compensation, but no such luck. I'd better go and look for work. I've been supervisor of naval grounds. The job is just for show, for I can't see anything from this far away. Then the republic came, so I transferred to the *Angkatan Laut*, the Indonesian navy.

In those days, the Indonesian navy paid me for five days a week only, the rest I had to make up on my own. A lucky stroke, sir, was that I began to paint. Using my specs. And these pictures go to Holland. I'll tell you what: A man in Apeldoorn, Holland, asks me to paint him a picture of his parents' farmhouse. This gentleman sends me a drawing: This here is a linden tree, this one is that kind of tree, and another, all trees in Holland. So I say to this gentleman: 'Say Rembrandt is alive still, would you ask Rembrandt to paint you a banana tree, a sweet potato plant? Rembrandt has no way of knowing those trees, couldn't paint them, same as me.' There are already 200 of my paintings in Holland. You know why? Me they pay very cheap. That's how I was living in those days with my seven children, from that.

I've got a friend in Holland who has a leg missing. He is very well off. There he gets compensation. I, too, fought for queen and country, but that country has given me zero. In *rupiahs*[4] it's barely enough to live on, barely enough not to die from, haha. What the Dutch government gives me, their compensation board, is free spectacles. But I have to go to the eye doctor. I won't. Why not? The moment they start on my eye, I go weak, I faint.

Do you want to know something? When I still had my two eyes intact, I was a marksman. But with this eye – who has pity on me? Nobody. Actually, I suffer, but I don't allow it to show. I live according to my own insights: He who gives to the poor lends

3   From the Dutch translation of Luther's hymn,

     which differs from the English version.

4   Indonesian currency.

to the Lord. They may strike me, but I'll turn the other cheek. The only thing they've got to do is stay away from my eye.

There are times when I see nothing. Even my own daughter, a this distance, who might you be? My own daughter! I'm a car with two headlights. Well, one of those headlights is broken. That car goes up the Puncak road, up into the mountains. Very foggy place. And the car battery is weak to begin with. What on earth can the driver hope to see in all that fog, with just that one little light? He sees little. That's just like me."

Damin

"I'm a grain of sand that slipped through the sieve."

Born "one Sunday evening in May of 1916" in the village of Ndoko near Blitar, East Java. Father was a landless laborer working as a hand on other people's rice fields. "We were poor. I never went to school. As early as age three, I went along to the sawa[1] to help out a bit."
During the war he was a romusha on the Sumatra Railway. Later on, he became a farmer.
People call him mbah ubi[2] because he sells sweet potatoes. He also owns a stand of rubber trees in Logas, Sumatra.

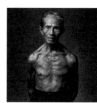

"Perhaps half a year after the Dutch surrendered, we heard that the Japanese were planning to construct a railway line to run from Pekanbaru to Muaro Sijunjung. The head of the village came to our house: 25 families in Nkodo had to give up someone, one person per family. I was the oldest, so my father thought I should go. Later on, they came to take away more people. The work was to last for three months, and after that we'd return to our village. They promised us that we'd be returning with fine clothes and lots of money.

We went to Jakarta by train and then on by ship. It started to get miserable on that boat. The crossing to Telukbayur near Padang lasted three days and three nights. The food was bad and we probably drank water that hadn't been boiled. Many people fell ill. Whenever anyone died, we'd roll him up in a mat and throw him overboard.

Altogether I was a romusha for over a year, maybe two. Many of my fellow villagers died, on one particular day four all at once. They went to bathe in the river after work around 6:00 o'clock and they had removed their loincloths: They were altogether naked. I warned them not to do so at the edge of the forest. Right after their bath, they got a fever and around 11:00 that evening they were dead, all four of them. People say the devil punished them.

Later on, I was in the hospital in Muaro, where they buried people alive. I saw with my own eyes how seven people, still groaning, were tossed into a hole. I've survived it all: Before I left Ndoko, my grandfather repeatedly blew a blessing over my head – phew, like that. Perhaps that explains it.

The first signs that the war was over we noticed when we saw the Japanese running away. Others just sat there inside their mosquito netting doing nothing, ruminating. And I heard that their commanding officer had committed suicide near the gold mine here in Logas. That's when I met some Dutchmen, who were planning to go back to Java. They were to take me with them, but that didn't happen. Why, I am not sure. Fighting had broken out again. Oh, yes, now I remember again. This time there was a war on between the Dutch and ourselves. That's why I couldn't come along.

Naturally, I wanted to go back to Java, but where was I going to get the money? My dream of seeing my family again was never fulfilled. I very much longed for my parents. But I couldn't write letters. Still, I was in touch with them in my thoughts.

I first got married to a woman from Logas. After two years we were divorced, and I married someone else. I am divorced from her, too. In 1969, I married for the third time, this time to a Javanese woman. That was much better. With her I went back a couple of years ago, but just to her village. I'm sure my parents had been dead long since. Maybe my two brothers were still alive at the time, but never mind. It would have been different had they been sisters, with whom you have a stronger bond.

I was glad to be there, but I saw how very difficult life was there. Had I stayed on Java, perhaps I would have been poorer than I am now.

1 Irrigated rice field.

2 Grandpa sweet potato.

We're reasonably well off here. These past five years, I've not been thinking that much about Java. Actually, only when I'm ill.

I often ask myself: Why has my life been so difficult from the time of my birth till adulthood? Only after independence did things improve, that's when you were free to come and go as you pleased. And how did I actually manage to get through those hard times? I got sick, but I got well again; we had so very little to eat, but I'm alive yet. All those people who died, in combat or otherwise, are like pebbles that got stuck in the sieve. I am a grain of sand that slipped through."

Dulrahman, nicknamed Sidul

"My gosh, to think that after 50 years
I'm still dreaming about that!"

*Born March 5, 1920, in the village of Tahunan in
the Gunung Kidul region near Yogyakarta, Java.
He was a romusha in various locations, finally on
the Burma Railway.
He is a farmer with just over an acre of land on
which he raises corn, cassava, rice and peanuts.
He also has some coconut trees and teak for
fences and firewood.*

"During the Dutch period, my father was a forester on an enormous estate of some 25 by 30 miles. There were seven of us, and I was the sixth child. From age seven on, I lived with my grandfather. He was a nose, throat and ear specialist in Yogya. That's why I could attend the Javanese school there. We didn't use the Latin alphabet but Javanese script instead. The school had a three-year program. This is about as far as people belonging to the lower classes would get. You could only continue your education if you were descended from the *kraton*.[1] So I went back to my parents and I assisted my father in his capacity as forester. Until the war came.

In June 1942, a Japanese by the name of Kawakubu came to our village and asked my father if there were any people who could work, for wages, of course. My father then gave him my name. They first assigned me to help build a tunnel at Parangtritis, south of Yogya, on the coast. We didn't get paid at all, however, and they told my father they'd kill him if he'd come to fetch me. Sure, the Japanese told us repeatedly: 'We've come to free you from colonial oppression.' But meanwhile they forced us to work for them!

We left from Gunung Kidul for Parangtritis with about 500 people. My estimate is that about 300 survived. It's hard to be precise, for people were not buried but simply tossed into the sea.

Some eight months later they shipped us out by the hundreds, including about 100 people belonging to the Gunung Kidul group. It turned out that they had taken us to Digul[2] to cut trees for building a road and a prison. Compared to this place, Parangtritis had been pleasant. There at least we got a piece of cassava the size of my fist, and we could fetch water from a small mountain lake. In Digul, however, we were left to our own devices and so we had to forage for ourselves. For food, you had to look in the jungle. We ate leaves, and any snake you'd find was good for roasting.

That lasted for three months. They promised they'd give us a present if we did really well. So I started to work extra hard. But I got nothing. And nobody got anything. We dared not make any demands, either, for fear of being killed. Many of us died there, including a lot of my friends. Especially because of hunger, but also because of bad treatment.

I already said: There were about 100 of us from Gunung Kidul who went to Digul. When we left three months later, there were 75 of us left. I was not exactly in good shape anymore, and that was true for most of us. Many of them were ill, but I wasn't. We were just skin and bones and we'd lost all strength. At first it took just four of us to drag a tree trunk, but toward the end it easily took 12 men to do so.

Finally, they told us we could go home. Everybody was elated. 'Things are already going fine with your country,' they told us. My parents received a batik cloth of the brand Becak, which I was alleged to have sent them, but I knew nothing about it. But about halfway, in the middle of the ocean, we began to ask ourselves: Where on earth are they taking us this time? There was no

---

1 The court of the sultan.

2 In Irian Jaya, a former Dutch penal colony in what
   was then New Guinea.

land to be seen anywhere. The voyage took a month. Sometimes it was quite scary, with high waves, and several times the boat couldn't continue because of engine failure. We finally arrived and got off the ship and that's when we panicked: Where on earth were we? This wasn't Indonesia, but then what country was it? This was certainly the case when we met people we couldn't understand. After one week, I found out that we were in Burma. That's what other romushas told us. And we asked them: Where then is Burma? Well, they didn't know, either.

In Burma, life for a romusha was terrible. But compared to Digul it was better. I was fortunate to have a Syrian for my supervisor. He didn't beat people, wasn't cruel. However, there were Japanese there, too, and if we did anything wrong, they'd beat us up vigorously with their rubber truncheons. That was no joke. If you got beaten with that truncheon it would remove your skin when bouncing back, and that caused a lot of pain.

This is where I had to dig away dirt and stones for laying the track. Once I was smothered by an avalanche of earth. We were digging a tunnel when, all of a sudden, the walls caved in and I was buried. People were lying on top of me and underneath me. I was, therefore, not directly covered with earth and still had a bit of room to breathe. There had been quite a lot of us, maybe 50 or so, and only about seven survived. After two days and two nights, they dug me out, using a bulldozer. 'I'm still alive, I'm still alive!' I cried. But all those lying on top of me were dead. I immediately lost consciousness after this and I didn't come to until a week later.

Whenever we'd come back from work to our barracks, I'd lie and think: How will I ever get home again? And where is home? I do not even know how to get there. Also, what am I going to eat? It was pure torture. There wasn't anybody without edema: We were all swollen, but not because of our good health. When you pressed into our skin, little marks would remain. It was all moisture. Everybody was

suffering hair loss, and later I heard that it had to do with malnutrition. Well, what do you expect, considering the food we got. What one man eats today, we had to share with the five of us.

During the day, while working, my thoughts went in all directions. I especially thought of my parents and my family. Would they still be alive, or had the Japanese maybe killed them already? And did the Japanese actually still rule Indonesia? It made it all more difficult. We often talked about our families, too. That made us quite emotional, and we cried. I really didn't have any hope left that I'd ever get free. Whether or not I'd stay alive or be murdered was something I left up to God.

I had a friend called Selam, who came from the same village I did. He was so without any hope at all that he simply gave up one day and died. Eleven of us had left my village of Parangtritis as a romusha. Four were either beaten or kicked to death. One of them died in Digul, and then Selam died in Burma.

The five of us were very sad when he died. Whether we wept openly or not, we all wept in our hearts. We didn't know either if or where he'd been buried, at sea or on land. He'd been wrapped in a cloth and the Japanese had taken him away in a truck. Following his death, the bond between the five of us only grew stronger. If you die here, then for all intents and purposes I will die here, too, that's what the mood among us was. We're all in this together. We tried to cheer up one another, especially by telling stories: Old Javanese histories and myths. One of us could tell stories from the *Ramayana*[3] well, another about the history of the ancient kingdom of Demak.[4]

I think every one of us had something special, a force that helped us to survive. One of us got tied up by the Japanese one day and kept under water for over five hours. His head, too. But yet he

---

3   Hindu epic.

4   The first Islamic kingdom in 16th century Indonesia.

survived! How, I couldn't tell, that I do not know. But after that the *mandurs*[5] were afraid of him. Furthermore, there were five principles we clung to: Honesty, obedience to Japanese rules, not being selfish, to conquer hunger with patience, and the belief that the five of us would return as one alive to our families. This came about after Selam's death.

We spent exactly one year in Burma. One of my friends kept track by putting little stripes on his arm. We couldn't bathe, so the stripes remained visible. One day, our Syrian foreman let it slip that we'd be going home in two weeks. He said: 'Don't tell the other mandurs I told you. But when you will all be back in your own country, then please let me know what has become of you.'

I didn't quite trust this news, thinking: For all we know we'll be killed now. However, after a month on board the boat, sometimes with high waves again, we arrived in Surabaya. From there, the five of us went back to Gunung Kidul. We tried to hitch a ride with trucks, but since we looked like a bunch of beggars or vagabonds nobody stopped. In the end, we began to walk: It took us 21 days.

When I arrived, everybody cried. They thought I'd been dead long since. I certainly looked quite different, because of the edema. During the first month, my family treated me a bit like a retiree, as it were. I was not allowed to work and they fed me very well.

The five of us, meanwhile, could think of nothing but revenge. We wanted to find that Kawakubu, the Japanese who had enticed us to come along with his false pretenses, and we wanted to make him pay. However, just then Sultan Hamengkubuwono IX of Yogya decreed that people could not take justice into their own hands. Vengeance was forbidden. And the sultan possessed certain powers. He could be in more places than one at the same time, for example. And if he should get angry with you and wish you dead, then you'd die, just like that and all at once. We feared him and so we abandoned our notions of revenge.

Because of all these experiences a person changes, naturally. Before I left, I had experienced nothing, let alone such a bitter experience as this. That changes the way you think entirely. I tend to think a lot more about things nowadays. I've learned to control myself. Anger only makes things worse. Through self-control you are actually able to prevent a situation from getting worse, from ever getting as bad as it was then.

I still dream a lot about those days, especially about the work we did: Dragging stones, that sort of thing. And about that voyage across the sea. Those high waves. That results in a nightmare once in a while, and then I find myself screaming out loud. Whenever that happens, my wife has to wake me up. Then she says: 'Better have something to drink first, and then tell me what that dream was all about.' My gosh, to think that after 50 years I'm still dreaming about that!

I still think about it a lot and I often talk about it with my children and grandchildren. At first they could not believe I had experienced such cruelty. They simply could not comprehend it. They couldn't until they had read books from the library.

I tell them these things so that they will treat other people well, not oppress or hurt them. Yes, and that includes the Japanese as well. Especially by reading Javanese books, I came to the realization that those dark emotions are no good. We are all brothers. Hostility among people only makes us weaker. And in the end, all that evil has still resulted in something good where Indonesia is concerned: Our independence."

5 Foremen.

Ngadari

"The terrible cruelty of the Japanese,
the torture..."

Born in Pengkok, Gunung Kidul district, near Yogya.
"I am about 86 years old." He was a romusha working on the Sumatra Railway, among other things.
Afterwards, he became a farmer. He inherited two
parcels of land: A rice field of more than half an
acre and two and a half acres of land in the mountains where he raises cassava, peanuts and soy
beans. He has two cows to plow with.

"The village council ordered me to become a romusha. The Japanese had ordered that every village
should supply a number of romushas, who had to
be young and healthy. There were 12 of us from my
village, and from the surrounding villages an incred-
ible number. I was about 20 and it happened on a
Friday, about four months after the Japanese invasion. Yes, four months after the bombardment on
Yogya, which I remember as if it were only yesterday.
On that day it happened to be our turn. They'd called
us together in the village hall, where right away
we had to get into a truck that took us to Yogya.
We barely had time to say goodbye. We didn't know
what kind of work we'd be doing or where. They gave
us a check-up in Yogya, and we got an injection
to boost our strength. A week later they took us to
Jakarta by train.

I stayed there for seven months. We had to
work on a railroad going to Merak, on the western
tip of Java. My job was laying the rails. We worked
from 7:00 till 12:00 o'clock, and from 1:00 till 4:00.
We were punished for everything we did wrong.
The cruelties of the Japanese were without equal.
They treated us like animals and beat us either with
their bare hands or with a rubber truncheon, the
kind the police have.

Following those seven months, they told
me I had to go to Pekanbaru. We crossed over from
Merak to Bakauheni, Sumatra's southern tip, a
two-hour trip by boat. From there they took us by
truck to Pekanbaru, which lasted a day and a half.
They did it in one haul, without stopping to eat.
The open truck was crammed full and it was the dry
monsoon: Terribly hot all the time, at night too.
We got nothing to drink. A lot of people got unwell,
they got headaches, and quite a few of them faint-
ed. I did not, but I got dizzy and I began to see
stars in front of my eyes, particularly because of
hunger and thirst.

We got two days of rest in Pekanbaru. They
gave us some rice, which we had to cook ourselves.
We drank the water without first boiling it. Sure,
that made your belly rumble – but what do you
expect, water that wasn't boiled! Even so, most
of us got better soon enough. Then they put us to
work. I had to saw rails into sections. That was
hard work, and the misery is impossible to describe.
Three fellow villagers of mine died there. They were
working on a bridge somewhere in the jungle. Two
of them had to carry rails. The one in front slipped
and the rail fell on top of them both. The third, who
was busy sawing nearby, also was struck by the rail.
Because I was working close by, I saw the whole
thing happen in front of my own eyes. I also buried
them afterwards.

Whoever was sick was taken to the hospital,
but that was exactly the place where people died.
I, too, was sick a lot, just like everybody else.
I started to vomit blood. I was thinking: Is this my
fate then? But that's when I gathered myself and
went into the forest to look for healing herbs, particularly leaves from the *jambu* tree. You had
to eat those leaves the way a goat does: You don't
pick them first but eat them straight off the tree.
That's how I got better. I had remembered this
from my native region: If you have that sickness,
you've got to eat bitter leaves straight from the
tree. Don't ask me why.

I saw a lot of people die. They died of a com-
bination of things: They were beaten severely, the
workload was very heavy, and there wasn't enough

to eat. People couldn't stand up to all that. And then they started to worry. I did, too. I was worrying all the time: Why do people get so little to eat, why do people have to walk around in these clothes made of rice bags sewn together with bamboo thread? Why do the Japanese treat us so badly? I'm living like an animal. The whole situation reminded me of the proverb *mundur ancur, maju tatu:* If you pull back you'll be crushed, if you go forward you'll get wounded. So I couldn't go forward or backward.

After 11 months, of the 12 men that had left our village only three remained alive. I began to panic. I was skin and bones and mentally I felt no longer able to withstand those terrible conditions. That's when I decided to run away, together with my two fellow villagers. Of course, that was dangerous. If the Japanese caught you they would kill you. In addition, in the jungle we could be eaten by animals of prey, and then I wouldn't even get a decent funeral. But it was much riskier still to stay, to be plagued by disease, hunger and poor treatment. I was not afraid, but determined. I kept thinking all the time how happy we'd be to get home.

At midnight, we fled the camp by way of the jungle, not the road. I prayed and asked for protection. That's all. I wanted to accept my fate any way it came. On the way, we tried to earn money for crossing over to Java. All the time we stopped to work: To plant rice, or harvest it, to plow, or to look after the animals. We had a hard time finding enough to eat. We went hungry a lot. I got so weak I just couldn't continue. That's when villagers gave us food, and I got some of my strength back. Sometimes we came upon areas where farmers used to grow crops and found cultivated crops gone wild such as bananas, cassava, and corn. We roasted the corn, but other things we ate raw.

One day we ran into a group of Japanese and that's when we acted as if we were stir crazy. We didn't say a word but just laughed a bit in a stupid way, while making strange movements. And we pretended not to understand a single word of Japanese. Those Japanese believed us and sent us packing, annoyed. What did I care that they thought we were crazy, for it certainly did save our skins.

After three months we could cross over from Bakauheni. We simply bought ourselves a ticket. Once across, in Tanjung Priok, we disembarked and started working once again to pay for our trip home. We arrived in our village 35 days later. Meanwhile, the head of the village had been replaced as well as the village council. None of the other romushas ever came back, not just from our group of 12, but also the eight that been taken a different time.

Whenever I think of those times, when I'm working in the field or before I go to sleep, the hatred of the Japanese returns. I think about it quite often, maybe once every two weeks or so: Their terrible cruelty, the torture all over my body, the lack of clothing and food, the friends who fell ill. That's when I get very angry. I can't explain it any better than that. When I don't think about it, then I'm alright, but the moment I remember I see the whole thing clearly before me again. If I were to encounter a Japanese, I wouldn't have to think twice. I only hope that my children and grandchildren don't have to go through anything like that. It's bad enough already for me to be carrying this burden. It is as if it clouds all of my thinking."

Ngadiyo

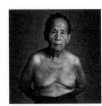

"Every day at least three of us died,
later on five or 10 easily."

Born in Gunung Kidul near Yogya in 1912,
"in the Javanese month of Suro."[1] During the war
he was a romusha in various locations, initially
in Singapore, later on the Burma Railroad.
His profession is that of farmer. He has his own
small parcel of land where he cultivates rice.

"Immediately after the Japanese had come, there
was a general call for young men willing to work
abroad. They didn't say what kind of work, only
that it was to be for three months. Thousands of
us left from Gunung Kidul. All I took with me in
the way of clothes and shoes was what I was wearing at the time. My pants, for example, were made
of some kind of burlap, in which we also bag rice.
I simply didn't possess anything else. First we
went to Jakarta. We stayed there for three months
and during that period we were split up in different groups. If during medical check-ups you were
consistently in good health, then they put you in
the group destined for Singapore. In Jakarta, we
didn't get all that much to eat. You could say your
belly was only half full. After three months, we left
by ship for Singapore. The voyage took seven days.
Everybody was seasick on that boat except me, so it
became my job to see to it that the others were fed.
In Singapore, we had to dig tunnels, among other
things. Every month we received two weeks' pay.
They told us the other two were held back to pay
for food, drink, a place to sleep, washing, sandals
and clothing.

    After a year or two, they told me I had to
work on the Burma Railroad. I was there for about
one year. When we arrived, thousands were already
at work. We had to repair the rail bed. It would
occasionally get damaged by flooding and land-
slides. Every day they took us by truck to work in
a different place, a ride of three hours at times.

It was full of mosquitoes and seven times hotter
than it was in Yogya. It was cold at night. Many of
us couldn't stand that climate. We got nothing to
drink during working hours. Our cooking was not
done the way it was for the whites. They had their
own cook, whom they had trained themselves.
The cook for the Javanese had no training at all.
We did receive injections to keep us in good health.
However, there was so little to eat that many people
died of malnutrition. If you added up the portions
for four people then you had just enough food
for one person. Others died of diseases: They'd get
dry beriberi, which made you shrink, or the wet
variety, which made you swell up something awful.
They'd get malaria. Or they would start coughing
up blood. Every day at least three of us died, later
on five or 10 easily. Out of the group of 200 men
that I came with from Singapore, maybe 70 men
returned alive. If you didn't work hard enough or
didn't follow orders, they'd beat you with a rubber
truncheon or with whatever was at hand. Not me
because I worked hard. They made me a foreman
of sorts because I set a good example. Although
I couldn't read or write, at least my body was
sound and healthy. That's why my workload wasn't
all that heavy. People who didn't work hard enough
got beaten on the head, so severely at times that
they died. The Japanese didn't always do this themselves, they also ordered others to do it for them.
I, too, had to beat other people. If I hadn't, I would
have been beaten myself. Not too hard, but enough
to teach me not to take pity on my comrades.
Whenever I struck them, however, I'd cup my hand,
making a hollow. That way I did not inflict much
pain, but it did make quite a lot of noise and that
satisfied the Japanese enough to make them laugh
out loud.

1   Suro is the Javanese name of an Islamic month.
    Because the Islamic calendar is based on the lunar year,
    the months differ each year from those of the Gregorian
    calendar used in the West.

I felt treated like an ox: Leave the stable early in the day to work without pay, return to the stable at night with just a bit to eat. If you did anything wrong, you got beaten. I found it very hard.

They took me back to Singapore after one year. We had to dig a cave up in the mountains. For five more months I worked there, that's when the Japanese went back to Tokyo and we returned to Java. The English announced that Japan had been defeated and that we could go home. Sukarno had said that the Javanese should return to Java. His government had made us work as a romusha and, therefore, his government would see to our return.

What I've gone through is an important experience in my life, but it hasn't really caused me any problems. I used to dislike the Japanese intensely, but not later on. I couldn't do anything constructive with that hatred, there was no way to vent it. Therefore it was better to be resigned. I have been blessed with a ripe, old age, so I've learned to accept it. Of course, I still remember everything but that is because we were not treated right. I think back rather often to those days in Burma and Singapore, at least once a month, and especially when I'm troubled. Or at night, before falling asleep. Until about 10 years ago, I still dreamed about working on the railroad. I saw everything clearly before me, as if it had been etched in my memory. That's when I slept poorly. But all of that is passed now. I wonder how things are in Burma nowadays. If I were still young and healthy, I'd like to go back to see if things are still as they were during the war, or whether they, too, are independent. The Japanese gave us our independence. How could I not be happy about that?"

Mohamed Nur

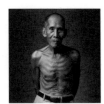

"Running away was dangerous, but so was staying."

Nicknamed Nur, born July 1919, in Menkoput, Meranbau district, Eastern Sumatra. "I don't recall the exact date anymore." Worked as a romusha on the Sumatra Railway during the war. He was a farmer who worked a rice field, had 10 coconut trees and some ubi, sweet potatoes. He also earned his living by fishing. He stopped working about two years ago.

"I attended grammar school till the third grade. Then I went to help my parents on the land. We grew rice and corn and I went fishing. But I don't wish to talk about those times for I don't really remember much about them: I only did pleasant things, played and helped my parents. Now I only wish to talk about the time when the Japanese held me as their prisoner.

In 1943 they came to the village and took 13 people with them. They included my father, my brother and myself. They told us we had to work on the Sumatra Railway and that we'd get enough to eat and drink. We would get 100 *rupiahs*,[1] no less, which was a lot in those days. But it was all a pack of lies. We didn't get any paid work at all. Work, yes, we got plenty of that alright. Boy, how we worked! Together with some 500 people from other villages and districts, they put us on the boat for Pekanbaru. Starting with that 14-hour trip, we got nothing to eat at all. And when we arrived, I witnessed three people getting shot. They had stolen some gasoline. I also saw the Dutch working in that dreadfully hot sun. They had to carry iron bars. They wore scarcely any clothes at all and their bodies were burned red. I took pity on those sturdy men slaving away in the sun.

We had to work very hard on the railway track: We had to haul dirt, saw wood, drag wooden logs and stack those to make a foundation for the railway itself. If we disobeyed we were beaten in our face and on our shoulders, or we were kicked. That's what the Javanese *mandurs*[2] did. The Japanese only came by twice a week. That's when they also beat those who couldn't work because they were sick. 'I am sick!' 'What do you mean, sick, you're lying!' And then they would kick you, and again, and I'd try to jump aside some. You could not defend yourself, after all. They had the weapons and power, and we didn't want to die, so we tried to avoid their blows. If we were very sick, we'd hide in the bushes by day. We hardly got anything to eat: Three times a day a little bit of rice with some salt and a few hot peppers. There were no vegetables. In exchange for our clothes, we ourselves bought *sago*[3] and ubi from the villagers nearby. How could we possibly work hard on a rumbling belly? We slept in a longhouse[4] of sorts. We'd light small fires underneath our bunks so that the smoke would drive off the malaria-causing mosquitoes. At night, we'd go to bed as soon as possible. Some of us would sing then.

We got sick, and there was no medicine, and many of us died, especially from malaria. Of the 500, maybe 100 survived. I lost my father and my brother. They disappeared and never returned. In order to fight malaria, I ground up some tree bark, mixed it with salt and water, and drank that.

After six months, only six of the 13 men from my village were left alive. That's when we fled, together. That was dangerous, but so was staying. I was sick and I wanted to go home. Before that I hadn't dared to run away for we didn't know just how far away from home we actually were and how many days walking it would be. If anyone were to ask after us, those who stayed behind simply said that we'd died. So many of us died, after all.

---

1 Indonesian currency.

2 Foremen.

3 Flour made of the pulp of palm trees and other plants.

4 Term used on Borneo for a home in which an extended family lives.

We first walked to Pekanbaru, 18 hours in all, and from there we went on by *sampan*. Its skipper said: 'Are you handy? Then come aboard.' He also gave us something to eat. After nine days, we arrived in my village. That's when I fell ill, and that lasted about three months. I got very cold, I shivered, and I itched everywhere. My mother took very good care of me. She washed me in salt water. And after that, I went back to work, to fishing especially. But I'd run away whenever I heard a boat coming. That's how afraid I was they'd come and take me away again.

I used to have this dream a lot of being grabbed and crying out for help. Then I woke up and went to wash my face. Those dreams have stopped a long time ago. I have often had to think back to the Japanese period, especially when I just woke up or when I was going to bed, and then it would take me quite a while before I'd fall asleep again. I always get angry all over again. Especially because my father and my brother are dead, thrown away. If I were to run into a Japanese now, I'd kill him. I'm no longer afraid. We're free now. Why then should I be afraid? I am sad, and I want revenge because my father and brother are no longer alive. If I hadn't experienced all of this I would have had pleasure in my work and in my life. Now I am sick, in my heart as well. I have little appetite and I remain restless.

When I heard that you were in Pekanbaru and wished to talk with romushas, I simply had to come. I borrowed some money and I took the boat; we left last night at 5:00 o'clock, my grandson and I, and we arrived this morning at 5:00. My son forbid me to go and said: 'You might very well die on the way.' And, of course, it does indeed cost a fortune to ship a dead body home. But my wife said: 'You'd better go. You're not going to die, no matter what.' I find it very important to talk about this, for other people have to hear about this. Particularly teachers, so that they may tell about this part of history."

Samlawi, nicknamed Lawi

"I've sent letters, but I'm not sure
if they ever arrived."

Born in 1914, 'I don't know on which date,' in the
village of Mandirancan in the district of Kuningan,
south of Cirebon, Java. His parents were poor
and they worked in a number of locations for what
we'd nowadays call public works. During the war,
he was a romusha on the Sumatra Railway.
He's been a farmer since. He cultivates rice
and he has a plot with ubi, or sweet potatoes,
and rubber in Pulau Arau, where his wife is from,
three miles from Talukkuantan, Sumatra.

"How did I get to be a romusha? Simply put, I got
cheated. I think it was in 1942 when the Japanese
came to our house, together with the head of the
village. I was made to come along. I'd just been
married for eight months and I lived in the village
of Jati, in the district of Tangerang, very close to
Jakarta. They told me they'd pay me a salary and
that it had to do with sport. Well, if that's what you
want to call it, go ahead, for it certainly had to do
with physical exercise, all that hard work. I could
neither read nor write, and they promised to send
me to school. They also told me it was just for a
three-month period; then others would go so that
I might return to Java. They took us to the sub-
district, together with another five men from the
same village; we didn't even get the chance to go
home to tell them that we were leaving.

From the district office, they took me to
Jakarta, together with another 66 men, and put us
on a boat. It was extremely dirty, for it was a coal
transport ship, and very full: Some 9,000 people
were on it. Chinese and white people as well. We
got rice with egg, which didn't taste very good and
probably was boiled in seawater. But you know,
we were hungry, so we ate it. As for something to
drink, we had to figure that out ourselves. Whenever
it rained, we tried to catch the drops. There were

also those who got water from the ship's faucet,
but I didn't, because it was salt water. A lot of
people died on that boat, including a friend of
mine. We were packed in there like ants, and I don't
know what happened to the dead. They must have
been thrown overboard.

On board that ship, I began to suspect that
I'd been cheated. We were told that we were headed
for Palembang, but the trip lasted far too long for
that. After two days and one night, we arrived in
Telukbayur near Padang. In Padang, they locked us
up in the local jail like criminals. The prisoners had
been let go before our arrival. Once a day, we were
allowed to walk in the sun briefly. For the rest we
just lay about, waiting for something to eat: Twice
a day a little bit of rice with an egg and every now
and then a bit of meat. For something to drink you
had to go to the well. Some of us drank it just like
that. Only God knows how long we have on this
earth, but I boiled it because I didn't want to get
sick. I was thinking of my wife. Yes, well, my wife
probably thinks I am dead. Many of us fell ill and
died, and yet again one of my friends died. And it
was my work party that had to bury them.

We stayed in prison for one week. Then they
took us in a train with blinded windows to Sawah-
lunto. We left at 6:30 in the evening and we arrived
the next evening around 9:00 o'clock. From there
we had to walk to Muaro Sijunjung and finally we
went to Batu Karyang in the jungle, where we had to
haul earth to level the terrain on top of which they
could lay the rails. The train couldn't hope to make
the steep grades either going up or down, of course.
Therefore, we had to raise the areas that were low,
while we had to dig away the mountains. And that
was very hard work. Day in, day out, without days
off. At six, they cried out: 'Time to work, time to
work, rise and shine.' We were, of course, hardly
fit and rested with all those mosquitoes and fleas
around. Everyone who could get up had to work.
If you didn't work hard enough, you were beaten.
And there was no breakfast. We got our first meal

at noon. It often occurred to us to flee, to get away from the Japanese and all that. However, we didn't know which way to go. We did know that if we were caught they'd beat you half to death. That's when you thought it might be better to stay put, after all.

There were also white forced laborers there. The whites used to have strong, healthy bodies, but now all of them were skinny. I did find it rather odd to see them working away just as hard as we did.

Our health situation was terrible. Malaria was the most common disease. Many people also had tropical sores. We had no medicine and the hospital was very far away. Some of us used herbs, but they didn't really know what they were doing. I was sick as well, but I always drank an extract from a bitter-tasting leaf, *daun kayu pahit,* which kept me healthy. It caused the mosquitoes to dislike the taste of my skin. I got malaria just the same. In addition to daun kayu pahit, I also drank an extract of *ilalang* grass,[1] which is also bitter-tasting. That's something you learn from your ancestors, something that passes from generation to generation.

I was a romusha for three years, from 1942 until 1945. I think I've survived because I always saw to it that whatever I ate was proper. And that whenever I drank, the water had been boiled. Some of us got so ill they simply drank water from the river. That only made things worse, of course.

One day, a Japanese car drove by with 30 Dutchmen in it. They said: 'We have won.' Our group consisted of only 25 men by then. We all made a run for it that very moment, me to Talukkuantan.

Naturally, I wanted to return to Java. My wife was there, but how was I to get back to her? I really didn't have a penny. I borrowed from Peter to pay Paul. Sometimes I worked on a rubber estate, then I would gather wood and sell that in the market. I did everything. Still, I never managed to save any of the money I earned. Then, too, I was a bit unsure. Maybe my wife thought that

I was dead and had remarried another? I used to lie there and worry a lot, especially before falling asleep. I couldn't sleep. I constantly would twist and turn, lie on one side, then on the other, thinking all the time. About Java. Of course, I longed for my wife and my family. I would weep at times, too, for I was very sad.

I've sent letters. I'm not sure if they ever arrived. But think about it, if a letter can't be delivered then they return it to the sender, don't they? And there's never been a letter that came back. So maybe they did receive those letters after all, but just didn't want to respond. I've sent so many, and I've never gotten an answer. I think that my family no longer wishes to know me, no longer wishes to see me. When I was young, my father always used to be angry with me. I always had to lend a hand and I couldn't go to school, the way my friends did. But if they don't wish to see me anymore, don't you think the least they could do is send me a note? I find it all very difficult, I feel cast out.

In 1947, I remarried, with a woman from around here, a widow who already had two children. Together we had another four. Please note, she paid for the whole wedding herself. I had nothing to offer but myself and my ability to work. I, therefore, considered it proper that I apply myself to the here and now. I never went back to Java.

But I still dream about it. As recently as last night. About my family, my brothers and sisters, about *wayang kulit* and *wayang golek*[2] and about my youth. I sometimes wonder: If I'd become an adult there, what would have become of me then? I was illiterate, of course, so I could only work with my hands. As far as money is concerned, I think my life

1   A long reed grass.

2   Wayang kulit: shadow play using flat, leather dolls, which are used to enact episodes from the Hindu epics Mahabharata or Ramayana. Wayang golek: puppet theater using wooden, three-dimensional puppets; mostly a tradition in Western Java.

would have been the same if I had been able to stay on Java. You understand that I've lived my life here solely to take care of our daily needs and to pay the children's school tuition.

I occasionally dream about the Japanese period: Bad dreams about all that work. I thought I gave it my best, but to the Japanese it never was good enough. And they themselves didn't do any work whatsoever, they just controlled us. The Japanese would always say: *mati bagus, kerja kurang, tidak bagus:* 'dead is good, isn't a problem, but working too little, that is no good.' That keeps recurring in my dreams. Also me sitting in that little train that falls over, and we all fall out. That's when my legs hurt, because we spill out all over the place. When I wake up, my legs are still painful and I have to massage them first. Isn't that odd? That's what I dream about, about something I never actually experienced."

Sardi

"I've had to bury my friend the way you would bury a water buffalo."

Born "probably in 1928" in the village of Candi Sari, Krobokan district, to the east of Semarang, Central Java. He was a romusha on the Sumatra Railway.

"After the war I've done all sorts of things. I was a farmer, I worked for a Chinese and I've been an civil servant."

"My father was a rice farmer. He died when I was still very young. So did my mother, when I was just in second grade of grammar school. My grandparents took care of me then. Later on, I started to roam the country. In the area where I lived, I would go from village to village to offer my services as a farm hand. After all, I had to feed myself, didn't I?

I was working the land in the village of Sumber Agung when the Japanese came. They simply plucked me and four others from the *sawa*[1] and took us with them to the Nawangan district. In Malay the Japanese told us that we had to defend the country. That's what I think, anyway. Because all I spoke was Javanese and no Malay at the time. All I could think was: What's happening? Will I manage to stay alive?

We boarded ship in Tanjung Priok and sailed across for four days and nights to Telukbayur near Padang. But it was not so bad. Only one man died and that was because he was sick. They threw him into the sea, with iron at his feet. I guess the misery started when I set foot ashore.

They took us to Logas, first by train and then by truck. I was put to work in Sarosa, some five miles from Logas. We were split up, and each group of 10 people had its own *mandur*.[2]

Things got worse as time wore on. The work remained the same, but the circumstances worsened. We had no medicine and we didn't get any pay at all. The food was bad: No rice, but *sago*[3] and cassava roots instead. And increasingly less of that, while we had to work very hard. The sick were not cared for and they got no food. Well, then they simply died. One of my friends got sick, and we were told to bury him. While he was still alive. He told us: 'I'm not dead yet.' We had to, though, otherwise they'd have beaten us with rifle butts, and we would have died ourselves. This was the most difficult thing I've ever had to do in this world. He was buried the way you would a water buffalo, that's what we call that on Java. If you bury a human being then you put him into a coffin or you wrap him in a shroud. Maybe my friends in Logas didn't tell you this? More people died than the number of railroad ties between Muaro Sijunjung to Pekanbaru. Nobody is as cruel as a Japanese.

After I had buried my friend alive, I went and sat down underneath a bridge. A whole day long, for I just couldn't go back up, all I did was sit and sleep. I couldn't eat, either. I was very troubled by it all. The next day, I went to the mandur to get permission to look for medical help. They'd usually grant such a request. Some would return, others would flee. I fled, to Talukkuantan. I had wanted to run away before, but I hadn't had the chance. Now there was this chance. And wasn't this a great deal better than being buried alive? In Talukkuantan, the *wedana*, the district chief, took me in. I told him my story, and then he let me work for him in the kitchen. About three months later, the Japanese surrendered. That's when I joined the Indonesian army to take my revenge on the Japanese. Because they had tortured us so much. But it didn't work out that way, and it hasn't until today: We had no rifles, and the Japanese did. So after three years I left the army, without any rights to a pension, that is, and I went to Logas because I had gotten to know

---

1 Rice field.

2 Foreman.

3 Flour made of the pulp of palm trees and other plants.

a lot of people there. That makes it easier to make a living. In Logas, I fell in love with my wife. We have nine children and 18 grandchildren. I've told them everything, including the bad things. They've got to know the whole story so that this sort of thing will not happen again. I also tell them: 'You've got to work hard and be diligent so that you will not be reduced to poverty and sadness and lead a miserable life.' I know what I'm talking about. Then they sit there, looking at me quietly, but they do follow my advice. Four of my grandchildren are already capable of driving a ten-wheel truck!

Did you see my little restaurant, in front of the door, along the highway from Pekanbaru to Talukkuantan? You can get coffee with cream there, and also *Indomie* [4] and a cool drink made with tamarind syrup. I've called it '*Ojo Lali*,' which means 'Don't forget!' So that my children and grandchildren and other people won't forget what I've been through and will work toward a decent future.

I'm not homesick about Java. When the war broke out, I was already without a father and mother and only had a brother. I'm still in touch with my little brother: We send each other a letter every month. But we've never seen each other again. Of course, I long for him very much. But I didn't have any money, and neither did my brother.

Because I worry a lot, my blood pressure is high. Just these last two, three days I've been bothered by this again. I get headaches then, and my vision is not clear: Everything shimmers. I often think back to the war years. I still do. Especially when I'm ill. I wonder how it's possible that I've experienced such misery and still didn't die. It's difficult to talk about, as if the whole thing gets stuck in my throat. Imagine me running into a Japanese now, I might want to kill him. But that will never really happen, of course. Ha! What Japanese would ever come to a village such as this?"

4   A vermicelli soup.

Sineng

"Not three months after the war the rails were already gone."

Born in Butu Leimo, district of Segeri, north of Makassar, Sulawesi. "I don't know when, not even in which year. I can't read or write. But I'm 96 years old. Just count backwards."[1] He was a romusha on the Sumatra Railway.
After the war, he served in the army for a year. He then started prospecting for gold and became a farmer in Logas.

"When I was 13, a Dutch family took me with them to Java on board a white steamer of the colonial government. I looked after the children, the *nonni-nonni* and the *sinjo-sinjo*, the boys and girls of the Dutch people. That's what I did till the Japanese came.

They picked me up off the street. My village elder had given people a mark, something red on one's clothes. This signified that you would be sent away. A war ship took us from Tanjung Priok to Padang, a seven-day voyage. At times we stopped in the middle of the ocean, and then they looked all around with their binoculars. From Padang, we went by car to Pekanbaru and from there to Logas: Time to start work.

My job was to haul dirt. Sometimes we had a pit or a hollow of about 10 yards that we had to level. We didn't have any big machinery to work with. Everything was done with a shovel. It would take me at least a whole day to tell you all about this.

Our food consisted of just *sago*,[2] no rice. Rice was certainly negligible. As to drink, we hauled water from the river, and whenever we had the opportunity we'd boil it, otherwise not. Many romushas died of hunger. We ate *daun kaju*, wood leaves, also called stream leaves. The Chinese use those a lot. If you don't prepare them just right they make you sick. They may be used to cure a pain in your stomach or aches in your muscles or joints. Whenever I think of those years, my heart becomes very sad. Things must be very bad when you're forced to eat leaves, don't you think?

There were bodies floating in the river. People were buried alive. There was this pit, and while they were alive still, they were laid down in there. But as I said already: An entire day would still not be long enough to tell you about this. I was still young, and my body was healthy and strong. I had rashes and stuff like that, but nothing else. Well, malaria, of course. That's when I pulled some *pitalo* plants[3] out of the ground, made an extract from their roots, and drank it. Terribly bitter-tasting. This I'd learned from the Dutch. While I worked for them, they also taught me the importance of cleanliness. Even if you have little money, it's important to keep yourself and your environment clean. The Japanese were the way we used to be, everything was dirty.

Very close by there were also Dutchmen working on the railway. They were beaten a lot, sometimes one man beaten by two Japanese. I could cry whenever I saw that. We Indonesians got beaten, too, but the Dutch were something different, something special. So whenever I saw them being beaten that way I got very sad. Then I'd rather just walk away. And, of course, I became very angry with the Japanese. I'm still angry, actually. It just doesn't show anymore. I only see the Japanese on television. Should I meet one, then... well. You can't very well remain angry with people like that, can you? What reason would you have? But, of course, you would like to get angry.

After the war, I was a soldier for three years. People said we had to defend our country, so that's what I did. I married after independence.

---

1 During the course of this conversation it appeared that Sineng was born in the 1920s.

2 Flour made of the pulp of palm trees and other plants.

3 Cassava.

My wife is from these parts, and this is where my children were born. Seven of them. One of them has died already. I used to tell them a lot about my romusha days, but not for the last 20 years.

So I didn't return to my family on Sulawesi. I wanted to build a better life. Before the Japanese came, I had nothing at all. Now I own a house. I built it with my own two hands. Right behind my house here were the railroad tracks. Not three months after the war, the rails and the wood were removed. By people from the city of Medan, so they say. That hurt a little, for a while. You've made that track with your own hands and then your own people take the whole thing apart. But to say that I think of those days whenever I leave through my garden gate: No, nothing like that.

I started prospecting for gold. I worked like a dog and I finally found some. That's when I bought four gardens with rubber trees. That's enough to live on. To say that I am well off: No. But that I am having a hard time of it: That not, either. There are people who are a lot worse off. In the old days, elephants would come to eat the young leaves off the rubber trees. Not anymore. Now it's safe around here. Where I'm from, from among the Buginese, life is hard, and they treat each other in a rude sort of way. And if I had stayed on Java... All I did there was be a servant to other people, while on Sumatra I became an independent farmer. Besides, things are not all that quiet on Java either, certainly not nowadays. No, it's better to be here. I've been living here for 70 years already. Well, something like that, anyway."

Witnessing the Elusive

A Personal Impression
Wim Willems

They are a marked generation, the Dutch who came from the East-Indies, a former colony in Southeast Asia. They have been marked by their struggle to survive during the Japanese occupation of World War II and by the civil war that broke out immediately thereafter. It was, however, not only the war that turned them into a society of people sharing a fate. Because of the colonial retreat, they also had to part with their country of origin or from the society in which they had lived and worked for so long. Within a span of barely ten years, between 1941 and 1951, their entire world was turned upside down. From being colonial citizens of the Dutch East Indies, they suddenly found themselves people trapped in a hostile, new country, an independent Indonesia. They were, to be sure, entitled to settle in the Netherlands, their other native country, but that move did take some doing. The Netherlands considered itself over-populated and did not always react empathetically to the arrival of these impover-ished compatriots from the former colony. Indeed, for a long time there was hardly any place in the Dutch national culture of commemoration for the war in Asia. The war in Europe domi-nated everything else, and it wasn't until the 1970s that people in the Netherlands became aware of what had happened to their fellow citizens overseas.

Half a century later, the traces of those dramatic upheav-als in Southeast Asia are still as palpable as they were back then. Even so, many stories about what happened in the 1940s have stayed within the circle of Indies insiders. People thought that outsiders would hardly be interested. This explains why those involved to this day get into heated and emotional arguments about getting their historical rights restored, getting their positions rehabilitated, or being compensated for their finan-cial losses. Judging by public opinion and media coverage, the country still has not come to grips with parts of the war in the Pacific. To this very day, survivors of the Indies episode still relive in their nightmares the indignities suffered at the hands of the Japanese and their collaborators and the loss of dear ones.

Also in memoirs, autobiographical documents and film documentaries the emphasis remains on the scars of horrors that never seem to come to an end. The Indies Monument in The Hague has come to symbolize such emotions.

The current image and self image of the first generation of people from the East Indies who returned to the Netherlands after World War II places great emphasis on victimization. Following the silence of the post-war period, the tales of heroism, and the therapeutic breakthrough in the 1970s, the cry for true recognition defines what seems now to be a new era. Hence the great interest in stories not yet told, disasters relegated to the footnotes of history, and the general sense of powerlessness among different groups. People who have walked around for a long time with an invisible past nowadays are demanding, indeed crying out, for recognition after all.

There's a danger, however, that the almost exclusive focus on victimization and recognition might result once again in a somewhat one-sided view of the war. It is precisely the individual stories that are snowed under as a homogeneous view is forged of a colonial past that in reality was dominated by sharp contrasts and different individual experiences. But this recent view based on victimization and recognition has become the standard that determines how one should cope with and provide information about war and violence. The nuances of the struggle, of survival, and of the human spirit disappear behind the images of bamboo fences, barbed wire, and the intense Japanese sun, which came to symbolize the suppression of Asia. The prevailing view apparently offers the first-generation of Dutch people from the Indies enough to identify with; it does so, too, for those from later generations who consider themselves war victims. Alternative accounts or different voices and images get pushed to the background because they don't fit the current established perspective on the past – a standard view that later generations have grown up with as well.

This fixation on the war and on the suffering within one's own circle of friends and acquaintances undermines the ability to have empathy for what has happened to others during those dramatic 1940s in Southeast Asia. The experiences of the Dutch community have become isolated from what happened in colonial society at large. That's why the experiences of Indonesian people seldom get much attention, nor do those of others involved, including English, Australian and American POWs. Such a narrow view makes comparisons difficult, which seems to leave no room for putting things in perspective, for humor or, indeed, for heroism.

This is not just true for the Dutch who experienced the Japanese occupation in the Indies personally but for Dutch society as a whole. The narrative of the Indies is about a lack of recognition and is hardly integrated into the national historical account of the 20th century, in which World War II plays such an impor-tant part. As a result, the Dutch population scarcely identifies with the overseas experiences of their compatriots. Various ethnic groups in Holland have their own collective history and memory. What happened in Europe seems light-years away from the events in Southeast Asia. Every victim places his own, unique experience alongside those of others. These differ-ent experiences invariably get treated separately in the media, in academia, and in politics. The usual explanation for this is that the different sets of stories and emotions rarely connect with each other because they are all the result of such different contexts and societies. This may be true on the surface, but a closer look reveals a great many similarities between the experiences of different kinds of survivors. The only way to break through this stalemate in the way we look at the past is to disregard people's different backgrounds.

With this book, photographer Jan Banning attempts exactly that. What is unusual about his approach is that he penetrates reality by introducing a perspective that allows for reconciliation. For both in his interviews and photographs, Banning has focused on the effects of war on people's private lives.

Most striking is how Banning looks at things. His photographs reveal the body as a metaphor for the legacy of the past. These are physical maps that trace the course of history. The war has left its impressions on the soul, and the body reflects those traces. Not just the pain, the horrors, the scars and the changed posture become visible but also the strategies that people have chosen, consciously or unconsciously, to leave the war behind and to continue life with a damaged past. We are essentially dealing with portraiture of the human condition in general. In it, various levels of strength and weakness, of doubt, arrogance, bitterness and heroism are recognizable.

The pictures show the men with a bare chest, the way they worked on the Japanese war projects. They're standing in front of a burlap background, a fabric symbolizing the connection with the years of occupation. The men reveal themselves naked, strike an individual pose, and do not hide themselves. They depict what has become of them, and the viewer may see exactly as much as he or she can comprehend. As a group, the 24 portraits reveal a reality from which one cannot escape. They form a multiple reality in which the specific and the general merge. Banning has chosen to portray white and Indo-European Dutchmen who during the Japanese occupation worked on the Burma Railway and on Sumatra's Pekanbaru Railway. In addition, he shows the bodies, hence the history, of the romushas – Japanese for coolie soldiers – Indonesians, in other words, who then were subjects of the Dutch East Indies. What all these men share are a place and an oppressor, which binds them historically and emotionally. Otherwise, they all differ in background, education, opportunity in life and experiences after the war. All those different lives have resulted in different textures on the one thing that all people have in common: Their naked body. The men have allowed those naked bodies to be photographed without reservation, which led to a penetrating and varied picture of what war does to human lives.

For the men who show their hands, the elongated fingers are striking, as are the veins underneath their paper-thin skin and the cared-for nails. Once, these very hands were covered by sores and bloody scratches, grit creeping underneath their nails. Now, they are folded together peacefully or they support a pair of arms that have lost much of their muscle. The hands emanate strength, tenderness and self-confidence. Some clench their fists, others hide their hands behind their back, while a few use them to keep their balance. They look like archeological objects on display in a museum. These hands look so real and sensual that it is difficult for the spectator not to touch them, however briefly, so as to share their history. Whatever doubt exists comes from diffidence, because the hands also serve to protect the self. These are proud hands that have been through a lot.

Also instantly obvious to the spectator is the variety in torsos. Behind that bare skin lungs hide that have had to endure quite a lot on the railways of the Japanese. Of some men the ribs show while with others they are hidden underneath the girth of old age. A few upper arms show a tattoo of a woman's face or a heart pierced by an arrow. Or simply the liver spots of the elderly. There's little in the way of body hair, there are breasts with sunken nipples or almost feminine shapes, as if to suggest that gender differences fade away as one advances in years. Like growth rings in a tree, the folds and wrinkles betray the men's age. Banning has photographed their skin closely enough to highlight every surface detail of their upper bodies. We see pigmentation spots, veins about to burst, and navels with a different shape on each individual stomach. We are dealing with the living texture of the human skin with curves, dark areas and parts resembling sandpaper. None of the torsos lacks strength, as is evident from biceps, sinewy muscles, or from shoulders with flexible contours. The outer skin of the upper body creates miniatures, fashioned by a photographer who has made it his business to portray human differences. He does so not by making a grand gesture but by painting the picture inwardly, leaving sufficient room for our own imagination.

Despite the emphasis on the bare chests, the spectator does not truly come face to face with the human mystery until he arrives at the portrait's final act: The head. The little details often make all the difference, such as a ring of stubble underneath the chin, an extended eyebrow, or a pluck of hair standing straight up. Then there's a drooping right eyelid, or a bundle of lines on the forehead that indicate tension. Some things seem similar, such as the many ears that look like giant shells attached to the temples. Ears are not easily hidden, which is precisely what makes them so vulnerable. Throughout the years they have picked up a great many languages. Apart from Dutch, Javanese and Malay, they've heard bits of Japanese, Bahasa Indonesia, and a scattering of western languages. What they have retained is impossible to tell. Human memory is like an untidy room from which all sorts of things disappear through the years. Loose-lipped or tight-lipped, each man portrayed keeps his mouth shut. Not one is showing his teeth, as if each man's character wishes to express itself without words. Because the eyes are photographed in black and white, and we are not distracted by color, their expressiveness is on display in full force. None of the men looks away from the camera. Their eyes reveal themselves as naked, the way their bodies do. This is the emotional heart of the pictures, which reveals the personality of each of the 24 men. We can barely comprehend what we see because it touches what is elusive, namely who we really are. We see a sad look, a shy glance, unguarded impishness, and inevitable gruffness. There's also amazement and resignation, a beaten look and serenity. We see eyes behind which we suspect violence, arrogance, grimness and vulnerability. But there are also faces that only emanate that one truth, that life is nothing but acceptance and resignation.

Jan Banning's portrait gallery is not intended as a documentary. We're not looking at the work of a photographer who set out to be a war correspondent. Rather his intention seems to be to trigger in us the desire for the stories behind the photographs. He wants us to end up at a rich variety of barely known histories in which personal fate and the general patterns of the past are interwoven. In the interviews, we witness a slight unveiling of the photographed men, one a touch more revealing than the other. The life of Banning's own father has been recorded here as well. It has turned out to be a sensitive portrait of a father daring to put his trust in a son who has clearly long since overcome his timidity. This personal touch adds something to the photographer's and the interviewer's attempts to visualize the long-term effects of the war. It does so to bear witness, not to accuse.

The reach of this book is, meanwhile, much broader than just the deposit of a near-autobiographical search. The book also tips the one-sided representation of the effects of war in that it reveals for each man portrayed an individual truth about his character, personal development and destiny. There's no escaping that a person is tossed into life as a solitary being. Everyone reacts differently to what life has in store for him. The men in these photographs could not turn their backs on the course of history and proved prepared to show its legacy. What they reveal is their authenticity. In so doing, they force the viewer to develop an independent view of a past that threatens to become set in stone.

Dr. Wim Willems (b. 1951) has written a number of historical works about Dutch people with an Indies background. Some of these are: *Het onbekende vaderland* ("The Unknown Fatherland"), The Hague, 1994, and *Uit Indië geboren* ("Born in the Indies"), Zwolle, 1997. His best-known book is *De uittocht uit Indië. De geschiedenis van Indische Nederlanders, 1945-1995* ("Exodus from the Indies. The History of the Indies Dutch, 1945-1995"), Amsterdam, 2001.

Acknowledgments

First of all, I'd like to praise and express my deep gratitude for the 24 men who were willing to expose themselves to provide insight to others. I found particularly admirable the contribution of the nine Indonesians, who, without the benefits of a society steeped in psychological exploration, had to respond to a line of questioning that to them was rather unusual.

Fortunately, an undertaking such as this attracts free and unsolicited support and counsel from a great many quarters. Naming all those involved would be impossible, but I'd like to single out a few. To begin with, Kees Arends felt compelled to offer a substantial financial contribution. Thanks also to Christine Maturbongs, who was most supportive, and to Will Tinnemans, a friend of many years who advised me on all sorts of things. I'm grateful to Esther Captain, Henk Hovinga and Wim Willems for the chapters they contributed to this book. Joy de Jong, Wim Roefs, Rion Verberne, Eileen Waddell and Suzanne Weusten all provided valuable advice. I'm very much obliged to Monique Soesman, who helped greatly with the organization of the Indonesia trip and interpreted the Indonesian interviews. Helpful, too, were Dick van Driel, Hilde Janssen, Rosa Verhoeve and Maartje Wildeman. For providing me with background information and contacts, I'd like to thank Makmur Hendrik, Gjalt van der Molen, Remco Raben and Fridus Steijlen. I was extremely happy with the help I got in transcribing the interviews; Siswan Mukharal, Judith Schut and especially Marianne van den Ende helped with this labor of love. Harry van Gelder deserves special thanks for his search for a Maecenas. Finally, I was particularly fortunate that my girlfriend, Judith Schut, so very kindly put up with my unrelenting fuss and bother.

Jan Banning, June 2005

Published in Great Britain in 2005
by Trolley Ltd
73a Redchurch Street, London E2 7DJ, UK
© Jan Banning, 2005
10 9 8 7 6 5 4 3 2 1
The right of Jan Banning to be identified as the author
of this work has been asserted by him in accordance
with the Copyright, Designs and Patents Act 1998.
A catalogue record for this book is available from the
British Library.

ISBN 1-904563-46-5

*Traces of War: Survivors of the Burma and Sumatra
Railways* (translated and adapted from *Sporen van oorlog.
Overlevenden van de Birma- en Pakanbaroe-spoorweg*,
Utrecht, 2003, ISBN 90-77386-01-7) is a production of
IF (Stichting Ipso Facto)
Begoniastraat 23, 3551 BJ Utrecht, the Netherlands,
phone +31.30.2448945, e-mail: ipso-facto@solcon.nl

This book and the photo exhibition by the same name
have been made possible with financial support from
the following Dutch institutions: Stichting Fonds Anna
Cornelis, Fonds Bijzondere Journalistieke Projecten,
Stichting Fondsenwerving Militaire Oorlogs- en Dienst-
slachtoffers (SFMO), Mondriaan Foundation, NCDO,
and Taxus Holding & Management BV (Bosch and Duin,
the Netherlands).
The english translation was made possible with financial
support from Stichting Het Gebaar and the Foundation
for the Production and Translation of Dutch Literature
(NLPVF).

The photographs for this book and the interviews
were taken and conducted between June 2001 and
April 2003.

Chief Copy Editor
    Will Tinnemans

Translation
    Frans Cateau van Rosevelt

Copy Editor English Edition
    Wim Roefs

Graphic design
    Peter Jonker

Maps
    Frank van Workum

Printing
    drukkerij Mart.Spruijt bv

Copyright photographs, interviews and introduction
    Jan Banning
Copyright historical introduction
    Esther Captain and Henk Hovinga
Copyright personal impression
    Wim Willems

✳ ✳ T R O L L E Y ✳ ✳